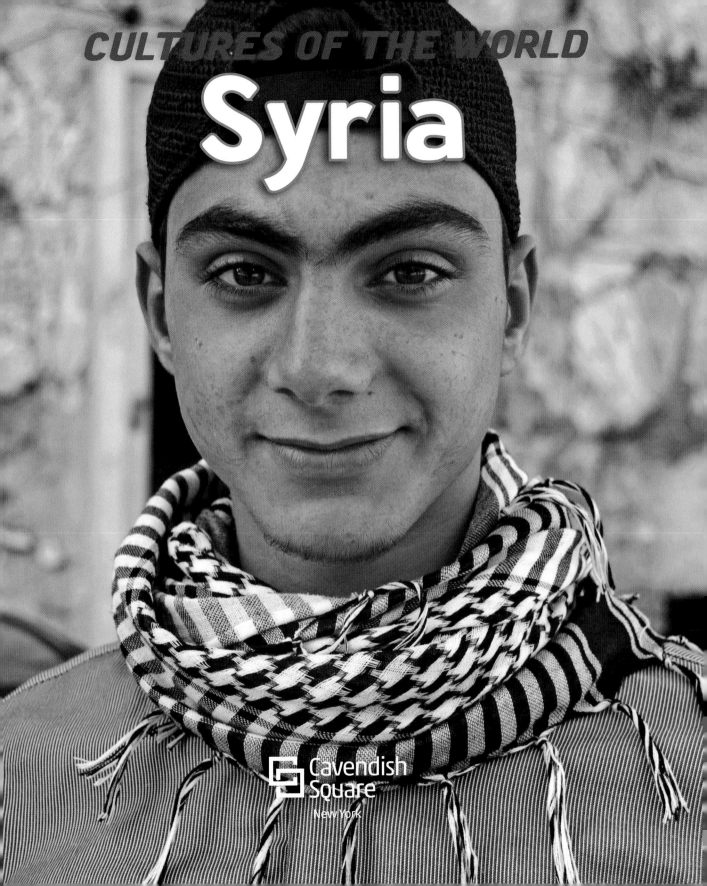

CULTURES OF THE WORLD

Syria

Cavendish
Square
New York

Published in 2016 by Cavendish Square Publishing, LLC
243 5th Avenue, Suite 136, New York, NY 10016
Copyright © 2016 by Cavendish Square Publishing, LLC

First Edition

Website: cavendishsq.com

This publication represents the opinions and views of the author based on his or her personal experience, knowledge, and research. The information in this book serves as a general guide only. The author and publisher have used their best efforts in preparing this book and disclaim liability rising directly or indirectly from the use and application of this book.

CPSIA Compliance Information: Batch #CS16CSQ

All websites were available and accurate when this book was sent to press.

Library of Congress Cataloging-in-Publication Data

Names: South, Coleman, 1948- | Jermyn, Leslie. | Spence, Kelly.
Title: Syria / Coleman South, Leslie Jermyn, and Kelly Spence.
Description: New York: Cavendish Square Publishing, 2016. | Includes bibliographical references and index. | Description based on print version record and CIP data provided by publisher; resource not viewed.
Identifiers: LCCN 2015050331 (print) | LCCN 2015049735 (ebook) | ISBN 9781502617040 (ebook) | ISBN 9781502617033 (library bound)
Subjects: LCSH: Syria—Juvenile literature.
Classification: LCC DS93 (print) | LCC DS93 .S66 2016 (ebook) | DDC 956.91—dc23
LC record available at http://lccn.loc.gov/2015050331

Writers: Coleman South, Leslie Jermyn, and Kelly Spence
Editorial Director: David McNamara
Editor: Kristen Susienka
Copy Editor: Nathan Heidelberger
Art Director: Jeffrey Talbot
Designer: Alan Sliwinski
Senior Production Manager: Jennifer Ryder-Talbot
Production Editor: Renni Johnson
Photo Research: J8 Media

Printed in the United States of America

CONTENTS

SYRIA TODAY

ONCE BEST KNOWN FOR ITS RICH HISTORY, IN RECENT YEARS, Syria has become one of the most talked about places on Earth. For five years, the country has been locked in the grips of a vicious civil war. The conflict has claimed the lives of over 250,000 Syrians and forced millions more to flee, creating the largest global humanitarian crisis since the end of World War II.

As the Syrian proverb goes, "A little spark can kindle a great fire." Following decades under a repressive government, in March 2011, protests broke out in the southwestern city of Der'a, just a few miles from the Jordanian border, when at least fifteen schoolchildren were arrested and tortured for spray-painting anti-government slogans on a school wall. The outraged community took to the streets, calling for democracy and the resignation of President Bashar al-Assad, the head of Syria's government since 2000. The peaceful protests quickly met with government-sanctioned violence. On March 20, more than twenty people were gunned down by security forces. For its early role in the uprising, Der'a became known as the "cradle of the revolution."

Hundreds of Syrians marched in support of the revolution through the heart of Damascus chanting, "Der'a is Syria!" in late March 2011.

To appease growing unrest, in April, Assad made small steps toward change, appointing a new cabinet and lifting Syria's emergency law, which had been in place since the Baath Party came to power in 1963. This law had given the government the authority to arrest people suspected of threatening national security, restrict public gatherings, censor the media, and track the personal communications of all Syrians. The president also disbanded the Supreme State Security Council, the court previously used to try individuals who challenged the power of the Assad regime.

Just days later, the government's violence against civilians escalated, with further shootings at protests. Government tanks and armored carriers rolled into several cities, including Der'a, Homs, and Baniyas.

The government could not silence the voice of Syrians, however. The violence against civilians had ignited a flame of revolution that quickly spread. By July, hundreds of thousands of people were protesting. Eventually, the protesters armed themselves to defend against vicious government attacks. As the fighting escalated, armed rebellion groups formed to fight the Assad regime for control of Syria's towns and cities. By June 2012, the United Nations (UN) deemed the conflict in Syria a full-fledged civil war.

There are countless reports of extreme violence and gross violations of human rights from all sides of the war. In August 2013, chemical weapons were used by the Syrian government in rural areas outside Damascus, killing hundreds of civilians. Countless more civilians have been arrested, tortured, and murdered.

The war has left Syria in a fractured state with a complex, constantly shifting network of battle lines and alliances. At present, the war is being fought between many forces: the Assad government struggles to maintain

control of Syria, while armed rebels work to bring new leadership and democracy to the country. At an ethnic level, simmering animosities have boiled over between the Sunni majority and the smaller Shia sect, which largely supports the Assad regime. In northern areas, Kurdish forces, a minority group long oppressed by the Syrian government, gained control of much of the northern border between Syria and Turkey. There, in January 2014, the Kurds established an autonomous region, Rojava, with the city of Qamishli at its center.

Amid these political and ethnic divisions, the civil war has seen the rise of several extremist groups, adding a further dimension of terror in both Syria and around the world. Two particularly powerful groups have risen to power during the conflict: the Islamic State of Iraq and the Levant (ISIL, also called ISIS, IS, and Daesh) and the al-Nusra Front. Armed conflicts between these

Soldiers in the Free Syrian Army prepare to launch an attack against extremists in the northern city of Aleppo.

Amid the fighting, several women representing some of Syria's minority groups joined together in Qamishli to celebrate International Women's Day in March 2015.

two enemies have left many Syrian civilians trapped in pockets of the country living under fundamentalist Islamic law. ISIL currently controls significant portions of Syria and large tracts of land in Iraq. ISIL has carried its acts of terror onto foreign soil, notably in the November 13, 2015, attack in Paris, France, which killed 129 civilians.

The presence of these terrorist groups at last drew in military intervention from foreign nations in 2014. In August, a US-led coalition, with the support of many Gulf states, began a series of airstrikes against terrorist targets in Syria and Iraq. In late 2015, France and the United Kingdom took a more active role in the strikes, launching their own attacks on terrorism. By December 2015, more than 2,700 ISIL-held targets had been hit in Syria. Another world power, Russia, a long-time ally of the Assad regime, also began airstrikes, with the supposed same goal of taking out ISIL strongholds. However, Russia has come under heavy criticism as evidence has shown that many of their hits have been in areas under control of the more moderate rebels fighting against Assad.

The war has led to one of the largest humanitarian crises of the twenty-first century. Over four million Syrians have fled the country by land and across the Mediterranean Sea to Europe. Millions more within the country are displaced from their homes and lack access to basic amenities such as water and food. Four out of five Syrians are living in poverty. The UN and other humanitarian organizations are struggling to provide assistance to the growing number of displaced Syrians with limited funding.

The war has touched every corner of life in Syria. Amid the wreckage, daily life goes on for the Syrians who remain. Many more have fled. The future of Syria remains uncertain as the country continues to crumble beneath the heavy hand of war.

Young Syrians play soccer at a refugee camp in Sofia, Bulgaria.

GEOGRAPHY

The snow-capped peaks of Mount Hermon rise high above the arid Syrian landscape.

1

SYRIA IS A LAND OF CONTRASTS. Cool breezes roll in from the west off the Mediterranean Sea, while hot, dry winds blow across the arid desert that composes two-thirds of the country. In this great sea of sand, lush oases stand out as life-giving islands in the desert. Vast mountain ranges cut across the country from north to south, creating a natural divide between the coastal plain and the steppe of the interior. For centuries, the geography and climate of this region have shaped the lives of those who make it their home.

Syria borders Jordan on the south, Lebanon on the west, Israel on the southwest, the Mediterranean Sea on the northwest, Turkey on the north, and Iraq on the east and southeast. It has about 110 miles (180 kilometers) of coastline.

The country is shaped somewhat like a triangle with irregular sides. It is about one and a half times the size of the state of Pennsylvania. You can drive between any of its borders in less than one day. Covering only about 71,500 square miles (185,180 square kilometers), Syria's strategic location has increased its historical importance to both

An aerial shot of Arwad, showing its harbor.

Middle Eastern and Western civilizations far out of proportion to its size.

Syria has one Mediterranean island, called Arwad, located just a few miles off the coast at Tartus. The island was an independent kingdom called Aradus in the days of the Phoenicians and contains many historical structures as well as a marina. Its inhabitants depend on fishing for their livelihoods.

MANY REGIONS

The western band of the country, where most of the people live, is less than 60 miles (100 km) wide and has a Mediterranean climate. The coastal plain is one of the most fertile on the Mediterranean. Temperatures here range between 70 and 90 degrees Fahrenheit (21 and 32 degrees Celsius) in summer and 50 and 70°F (10 and 21°C) in winter. In the desert, temperatures soar to 110°F (43°C). It is humid on the coast, with annual rainfall averaging 38 inches (96 centimeters).

To the east is a range of limestone mountains called the Jabal al-Nusayriya, which is cool in summer, and often snow-covered in winter. Between this range and the next is a drier but still fertile valley called the Ghab Depression, which was filled with marshes until modern times. Farther east is a range of dry mountains. The climate around this eastern range is similar, but with warmer summer temperatures and colder winter temperatures than on the coast.

The narrow strip of land along the eastern slopes of the coastal mountains is where the largest cities are, and the climate varies quite a bit from south to north. For example, the average rainfall in Aleppo, in the north, is about 18.5 inches (47 cm) per year but only 9 inches (22.8 cm) in Damascus, farther south. The rainfall increases again south of Damascus. The temperatures along this strip range from over 90°F (32°C) in summer to below freezing in winter.

The reason for the drier area around Damascus is the Anti-Lebanon Mountains. The western spine of this range is in Lebanon and is higher than

The area east of the populated strip, with the exception of some mountainous land along the Turkish border and the irrigated land along the three main rivers, is high steppe and rocky, gravel desert. The Syrian Desert, as it is named, also covers a large part of southern Syria, as well as eastern Jordan, western Iraq, and northern Saudi Arabia.

the coastal mountains of Syria. The eastern spine is higher yet and turns northeastward at Damascus. They end in the geographic center of Syria, east of Palmyra, and block most rainfall.

The triangle of land northeast of the Euphrates and Khabur Rivers is called Al-Jazirah (zha-ZEER-a) and is not as dry as the central desert. It gets about 10 inches (25.4 cm) of rainfall annually. Although most of the central and southern desert is 0.5 miles (0.8 km) or more above sea level, Al-Jazirah's altitude is around 1,200 feet (360 m). This area was part of ancient Mesopotamia.

The fertile soil of the Ghab Valley brings prosperity to farms sheltered beneath the mountains.

WINDING WATERWAYS

There are several large rivers running through Syria. The Euphrates, at 1,700 miles (2,800 km) long, is the largest river in western Asia. It begins on the Anatolian Plateau in eastern Turkey and joins the Tigris River at Basra in southern Iraq, where the two rivers create vast marshlands. Turkey has 40 percent of the river's length inside its borders. While Syria houses only 15 percent, this small portion has supported civilization in eastern and northern Syria for thousands of years. Although the river is quite wide—in

Throughout the Middle East, sandstorms are common during the spring months. Haboobs, the Arabic word for "violent winds," form when loose sand particles are picked up by a steady wind. Smaller storms can occur with winds traveling as low as 20 miles per hour (32 kilometers per hour). Larger, more destructive storms encompass wind speeds of up to 60 miles per hour (97 kmh) and can travel much farther distances. These violent

storms are extremely dangerous, resulting in poor visibility and stinging sand that can leave burns on the skin. In September 2015, a large storm swept across Syria and struck Damascus, killing three people and hospitalizing over three thousand. In the provinces of Hama and Idlib, fighting was forced to a halt while the storm blew.

some places nearly 1 mile (1.6 km)—it is mostly shallow with constantly shifting sandbars, and ships cannot navigate it.

The Al Balikh River also starts in Turkey, enters Syria in the north, and flows into the Euphrates in north-central Syria. The Khabur begins in the northeast and flows into the Euphrates at Deir ez-Zor, about 100 miles (160 km) from the Iraqi border.

The Barada is a small river that creates the Al-Ghuta Oasis, where the capital city of Damascus lies. The Barada begins in several mountain springs near Damascus and flows northeastward. Although it nearly dries up in the dry season, it has allowed people to live in Damascus for thousands of years.

The Orontes has its sources in Lebanon, flows northward through the Ghab Depression into Turkey, and then empties into the Mediterranean. Dams at Homs and Hama on the Orontes have made western Syria agriculturally productive and provided local industry with hydropower.

LIFE-GIVING OASES

Water is perhaps the most precious resource in the arid Middle East. Some of the things that have made life possible in this part of the world are oases. These are lowland places where natural springs surface and allow plants to grow. The most common plants are date palms, but some oases grow bananas and olives as well. Many of the palm trees are centuries old.

There are always small settlements around the water sources, some of them thousands of years old. In the past, these settlements served as caravansaries—resting places for camel caravans.

The spring water is channeled by small canals through plots of land that are often surrounded by ancient adobe walls 6 to 8 feet (2 to 2.5 m) high. These canals may have been the world's earliest irrigation systems.

The biggest and best-known oasis is the one at Tadmor, near the ruins of Palmyra. This oasis was the source of life for the ancient Roman city.

INLAND SEAS

Syria has several natural lakes. The most well-known are Al-Jabbul and Lake Ram. Others were created by dams built for irrigation and electrical power. One of the biggest natural lakes is Lake Ram, which fills the crater of an extinct volcano in the Golan Heights. As of 2016, the lake, however, was drying up. Al-Jabbul is the largest natural lake in Syria, covering 60 square miles (155 sq km). Another natural lake is Mzerib, northeast of Der'a, which is on the border with Jordan.

The largest artificial lake is Al-Assad, created by the Tabaqah Dam. The second largest lake is Qattina, southwest of Homs. This is the main source of the Orontes River, and although it used to be rich with fish, it is now badly contaminated. Another lake, about one-third the size of Qattina, is Al Rastan, formed by a dam on the Orontes River about 12 miles (20 km) north of Homs. About 9 miles (15 km) north of Hama is Lake Karma, another source of water for the Orontes. Lake Baloran, in the mountains northeast of Latakia, was created by a dam on the river of the same name. Finally, Lake Karn is a tiny lake in the mountains west of Damascus, formed by a dam on the Barada River.

URBAN CENTERS

Most of Syria's population lives in cities. Syria's cities have many modern elements side-by-side older neighborhoods. Some have narrow, winding streets, and many buildings have not changed in hundreds of years.

Damascus is one of the oldest continuously inhabited cities in the world. Old Damascus lies on the southern bank of the Barada River. One of its most famous landmarks is the Omayyad Mosque, which was constructed in 705 CE. Modern Damascus extends north of the Barada. It has wide avenues, large apartment buildings, and tall office complexes. The University of Damascus sits on the outskirts.

Syria's largest urban center is the northern city of Aleppo.

THE GOLAN HEIGHTS

For nearly fifty years, the Golan Heights have been a heavily disputed geographical region located between Syria and its western neighbor, Israel. The Golan is a high plateau bordered to the west by the Sea of Galilee and the Jordan River, and to the east by the Yarmuk River. At the northern end lies Mount Hermon, the highest point in Syria, at 9,232 feet (2,814 m). The Golan is shaped similar to a boat, with a wide middle and narrow ends. It runs approximately 44 miles (71 km) from north to south, and is about 27 miles (43 km) at its widest section.

Israel gained control over the Golan in the last days of the Six-Day War in 1967. Syrian forces tried—unsuccessfully—to retake the area in 1973. A UN-monitored buffer zone was established in May 1974 to monitor a cease-fire. It continues to operate today. In 1981, Israel annexed the Golan; however, this appropriation has never been recognized by Syria or the international community.

The geographic location and features of the Golan make it a strategic vantage point for whichever country controls it. The Syrian capital of Damascus, only 40 miles (60 km) away, and other southern areas are visible from the plateau, which allows Israel to monitor Syrian activities. The rugged, rocky terrain also acts as a natural defense against any attack.

The area continues to be disputed. Syria wants to reestablish control of the area based on the border dating back to before 1967. For Israel, the Golan and surrounding area play a vital role in providing one-third of the country's water supply. If the pre-war border were to be reestablished, this would give Syria control of the Sea of Galilee—the Israelis' much-needed main source of fresh water. There is also a large community of Israeli Jews who have called the Golan home since the late 1960s with strong ties to the region.

As Syria descended into civil war in 2011 and with the ongoing struggle for power over the country's leadership, the dispute over the Golan remains unresolved. As of 2014, there were about forty-two Jewish settlements in the area.

THE DAMASK ROSE

For centuries, the damask rose had been considered a symbol of love and beauty. These pink blossoms, which can stand over 7 feet (2.1 m) high, can be found in most gardens across Syria. It is believed that the damask rose was brought to Europe during the eleventh century by the crusader Robert de Brie.

In cooking, the floral notes of rosewater are used to flavor meats, yogurt, jams, and other delicacies. The rose's fragrant pink blossoms are also harvested as rose oil, a highly prized ingredient used in perfumes. Rose oil is also believed to have calming properties, which aid depression and stress.

Aleppo is also an ancient city, with the earliest settlements dating from about seven thousand years ago. A large twelfth-century Arab fort dominates the older part of the city. Modern Aleppo is a commercial and industrial center. Homs, a heavy industry center, and Latakia, the country's main port on the Mediterranean, were both established by the Greeks around 300 BCE.

THE NATURAL LANDSCAPE

Along the coast and in the coastal mountains, grapevines and pine, olive, and fruit trees are abundant. The cities east of the coastal range have green belts around them where most of their fruit and vegetables have traditionally been grown. This is changing, though, with a fluctuating population. Larger cities now import most of their produce from rural areas farther away. In and around Damascus, Homs, Hama, and Aleppo, there are olive, eucalyptus, pine, locust, maple, fig, palm, and citrus trees, and also many grapevines. Poplars and cottonwoods grow along the rivers on the eastern side of the coastal mountains, and of course, palm trees grow in desert oases and on the edges of the desert. In the cities, jasmine, bougainvillea, orange blossoms, and other flowers provide splashes of color and sweet scents during spring and summer, until the rising heat causes the bright blooms to wither and die.

WILDLIFE

Scorpions, lizards, and snakes are common in the deserts. Less than a century ago, gazelles, lions, eagles, buzzards, jackals, red foxes, desert hares, and wolves were also common. In medieval times, Arab princes used to fight lions as part of their coming-of-age ritual. They also staged large hunting expeditions for desert creatures.

Sadly, it seems that most larger wildlife in Syria is already gone or on the way to disappearing. The few animals that remain—gazelles and foxes, for example—are still hunted for sport.

There are several reasons for the disappearance of the wildlife. One is human population growth and its encroachment into all fertile areas of the country. Another is the use of DDT and other poisons that are banned in most Western countries. Yet another is the wild dogs in the desert, kept by Bedouins to protect their sheep. These fierce animals often run in packs and will even attack people. Fragile desert ecosystems are easily disrupted by such human activity and by the introduction of non-native species.

Another reason may be climate change. Over the past few centuries, a lot of land that used to be fertile has become desert. In the central desert, for example, there are ruins of Arab palaces once used as hunting lodges. To build and use such permanent structures required regular supplies of food, water, and fuel, none of which are available there now.

The Syrian hamster, also called the golden hamster, was discovered near Aleppo in 1797. This tiny rodent is vulnerable in the wild.

INTERNET LINKS

countrystudies.us/syria/19.htm
An overview of the geography of Syria from the US Library of Congress.

www.jezreelvalleyregionalproject.com/geography-of-the-levant.html
Learn about the history and geography of the Levant, including Syria.

HISTORY

This prehistoric bowl dates from about 4500 BCE.

2

Syria has been
nicknamed
the "cradle of
civilization" because
of its rich history.

FOR CENTURIES, SYRIA HAS SERVED as the crossroads of many great civilizations. For over seven thousand years, the ancient mountains and arid desert of the Syrian landscape have born witness to the rise and fall of many great peoples and empires. During the twentieth and twenty-first centuries, the question of who controls this ancient land has once more been called into question.

FROM ANCIENT TIMES

The earliest prehistoric remains of people found in Syria are from the Middle Paleolithic period. Fertility goddess statues and flint and obsidian tools of early peoples have been found in Ugarit, on the Syrian coast.

A thousand years later, settlers began using primitive soft pottery. Then, four thousand to five thousand years ago, ceramics in elegant shapes, painted with geometric designs, began to appear. The technology of the pottery slowly improved, and during the first millennium BCE, copper work appeared.

FROM THE WEST

Around 2000 BCE, the Canaanites moved onto the coastal plain and the seaward side of the coastal mountains in what is now Israel, Lebanon,

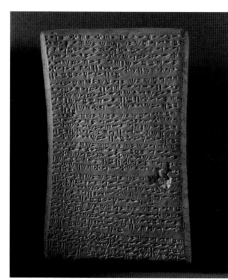

A tablet inscribed with Ugaritic text, dating from about 1300 BCE.

and Syria. These people were called Phoenicians by the Greeks. This name referred to all the peoples of the area, although none of them called themselves by that name.

Phoenicians were the first great seafarers, establishing colonies and trading with people all around the Aegean Sea. It was during their time that the already ancient settlement at Ugarit was given its name. They developed and improved iron tools and had the first royalty that wore purple robes. The purple dye came from a mollusk unique to the Mediterranean shores of Syria. The first known kings were Niqmadou and Yaqaroum. During the fifteenth century BCE, the Egyptians invaded and conquered parts of Syria but left the Canaanite kingdom intact; the two groups were friendly.

The earliest known alphabetic writing dates from the reign of Niqmadou II (circa 1360—1330 BCE). The writing, in alphabetic cuneiform on tablets, tells much about the customs and institutions of the coastal people. The tablets show that the Canaanite kingdom included a large part of what is now northwestern Syria. They speak of extensive diplomatic activity to safeguard the kingdom from the advance of both the Egyptians on the south and the Hittites on the north.

Thereafter, trade, war, and political intrigue became increasingly common among the peoples at this end of the Mediterranean, and Ugarit was finally destroyed around the end of the thirteenth century BCE. The city never rose again, but during the fifth and fourth centuries BCE, Greek fishermen built some dwellings there, atop a hill that covered thousands of years of buried history, and named the place Leukos Limen.

FROM THE EAST

Around 3000 BCE, the ancient Sumerians (of what is now southern Iraq) spread northeastward into what is now eastern Syria and northern Iraq, eventually occupying most of the land between and around the Euphrates and Tigris Rivers. The area is often referred to as Mesopotamia, the Fertile Crescent, and Babylonia. The people became known as Babylonians. Mari, an archaeological

The development of written language may be the most significant aspect of Syrian history. There were two original types of writing: the hieroglyphic style of Egypt and the alphabetic cuneiform style discovered at Ugarit and in ancient Sumer. Cuneiform was the simplest, consisting of only thirty shapes, one for each letter. The Phoenician alphabet was later used as the basis for Greek, which in turn was the basis for most Western alphabets. Arabic also has its roots in Ugaritic.

The language represented by cuneiform characters—called Ugaritic—was one of several languages used in Ugarit. It was spoken by most of the city's population and was used in poems and myths. Babylonian, the international language of the time, was used in diplomatic correspondence and judicial documents. Most of the texts found are in these two languages—Ugaritic and Babylonian—but others have been found in Hurrian (a non-Semitic language of eastern Asia Minor), Cypro-Minoan, Hittite, and Sumerian cuneiform, and Egyptian and Hittite hieroglyphics.

site on the Euphrates River near the Iraqi border, has turned up evidence of settlers as far back as the second century BCE. In 1933 CE, the remains of a three-hundred-room palace were uncovered here—one of the biggest palaces ever discovered!

At the same time that the Babylonians were developing and expanding, the civilization of the Assyrians was developing on the northern Tigris River. The Assyrians, from whom Syria got its name, were as well known for their military conquests and brutality as the Babylonians were for their accomplishments in science, the arts, and religion.

In 2300 BCE, a group of Semitic people under a leader known as Sargon conquered Babylonia and established the kingdom of Akkad. Not long after, this kingdom fell to Guti tribes from the Zagros Mountains between modern Turkey and Iran. In the nineteenth century BCE, Amorites, descendants of the Canaanites, conquered the region. The Assyrians took over all of Babylonia in the fourteenth century BCE. A hundred years later, they had occupied most of Syria and Phoenicia. In the tenth century BCE, however, the Aramaeans drove them back.

MIGHTY EMPIRES

In the eighth century BCE, the Assyrians returned and conquered all of Syria, ending the area's divided history. However, this empire did not last long. In the seventh century BCE, King Nebuchadnezzar led the Babylonians to conquer the land. A hundred years later, Syria became part of the Persian Empire. Then, in 333 BCE, Alexander the Great conquered it, and it remained a Greek outpost until the Romans, under Pompey, added Syria to the Roman Empire in 64 BCE.

The period of Roman rule was prosperous, and much building was accomplished. The Romans left the largest number of remains in Syria: cities, amphitheaters, temples, and forts from Turkey to Jordan and from the Mediterranean coast to the Euphrates River. Damascus became famous for its architecture and its schools of law and medicine. Palmyra, a trading center for caravans, reached its height in the mid-third century CE.

In 395 CE, the Roman Empire split in half. Syria became part of the eastern, or Byzantine, empire. The Byzantine rulers, who were Christian, tried to convert the Syrians but were successful only in the north.

There were three Roman emperors who came from Syria. One was Philip, who ruled the empire from 244 to 249 CE. His birthplace of Shahba has ruins of a Roman theater, Roman baths, and a museum of well-preserved mosaic floors. The other two emperors, Alexander (Lucius) Severus (193–211), and Elagabalus (218–222), came from Homs (called Emesa at that time), 100 miles (160 km) north of Damascus.

THE QUEEN OF PALMYRA

Smack in the middle of Syria, about 150 miles (241 km) from the nearest city, stand the ruins of Palmyra, an extensive and beautiful Roman city that was built in the early third century CE. In 260 CE, a man named Odenathus was given the title "king of Palmyra" by the Roman emperor. His wife's name was Zenobia, and little is known about her before she married him, except that she was one of the best-educated women of her time and was an expert linguist. There are rumors that she was half Arab and half Greek—but this has not been confirmed.

On its reign of terror, ISIL has set out to destroy many of Syria's oldest ruins, annihilating any history not related to the Islamic faith. The ancient city of Palmyra is one of the sites that has experienced the most destruction.

Nicknamed the "Venice of the Sands" and the "Bride of the Desert," the ruins of Palmyra were named a world heritage site in 1980 by the United Nations Educational, Scientific, and Cultural Organization (UNESCO). The world-famous archaeological site once drew more than 150,000 visitors each year.

In May 2015, the war reached Palmyra when the historic site fell under the control of ISIL. While Palmyra's ancient ruins had survived for centuries, many have now fallen at the hands of terrorists. The extremists have destroyed many of the site's prized structures, including the Temple of Baal Shamen and the Temple of Bel. They have also looted countless artifacts to sell abroad on the black market.

To protect Syria's ancient artifacts from further looting and destruction, a team of 2,500 people, known as the "Monuments Men," are working to transport artifacts from sites across Syria to the National Museum in Damascus for safekeeping.

Odenathus died in 267, and it is suspected that Zenobia had a hand in his death. Zenobia proclaimed herself queen, although she was officially acting as regent for her baby son. For a while, she appeared to defend Roman interests in the area, but starting in 268, she embarked on a conquest for herself. Her armies took over all of Syria, ventured into Egypt in 269, and by 270 had conquered all of Asia Minor, building fortifications at strategic points to defend her realm. In 270, Aurelian was elected the new Roman emperor, and at about the same time, Zenobia proclaimed her still-infant son, Septimius Vaballathus Athenodorus, emperor.

This painting depicts Queen Zenobia's final look back at Palmyra before she was captured by Roman troops.

Aurelian became alarmed at the ambitions of Zenobia and sent a trusted general to recapture Egypt. He himself went after the queen of the desert, defeating her army in Antioch (now Antakya, Turkey) and at Emesa (now Homs, Syria) in 271. He then reached Palmyra, which Zenobia defended for some time, but the city eventually surrendered and was razed by his troops in 273.

Legend claims that Zenobia and her son were captured by Roman soldiers as they fled Palmyra, and when the soldiers wanted to kill her, she saved her life by blaming her ministers and allowing them to be executed in her place, including one who had been her linguistic tutor. Whatever happened, Aurelian marched triumphantly back to Rome in the year 274 with the rebel queen in tow on a golden chain, bound with golden shackles and covered with expensive jewelry. Some say she married a Roman senator and lived out the remainder of her life in a villa at Tibur (now Tivoli). Aurelian also pardoned Zenobia's son and married her daughters into influential Roman families.

Zenobia is an important figure for many Syrian women. When Syrian men say a woman should only do certain kinds of work, that she cannot lead a country or an army, many women counter with, "What about our Queen Zenobia?" Even though her reign was short, she challenged the world's largest empire and held off its armies for several years. Perhaps equally important, she was successful in defeat, earning the respect of the very people she had tried to outdo.

THE OMAYYAD DYNASTY

Although all of the civilizations and empires left their mark on Syria in some way, it was the zeal of Islam that changed it permanently and formed the basis of modern Syrian society.

After the Prophet Muhammad's death, his followers were divided over who should lead them. The Shia Muslims argued that it must be a member of the Prophet's family and chose Ali, the Prophet's son-in-law. The majority of followers, the Sunnis, wanted to elect caliphs to rule in his place. Immediate animosity developed between the two groups and continues today.

In addition to this split, there were conflicts between clans struggling for political and religious power. The Omayyads were initially the strongest of these clans. Led by Khalid ibn al-Walid, they conquered Damascus in 636, and most of the population adopted Islam as their religion.

The Omayyads ruled most of the Arab empire from Damascus, from the mid-seventh to the mid-eighth centuries. They continued in their drive to spread Islamic rule and eventually extended the Arab empire to include the entire Arabian Peninsula, northern Africa as far as the Atlantic Ocean, and southern Europe—an area about the same size as the former Roman Empire.

After the Omayyads took over in the seventh century CE, Arabic spread as the common language of the land. Although Christianity had strongholds in the mountains of western Syria, the only religion that was able to take hold uniformly was Islam, and it has had an overriding influence on the country's development and direction ever since. Adherents of other religions were, however, allowed to continue to practice their religion.

The Omayyads built roads, founded hospitals, and encouraged education. Scholars from other lands studied in Damascus, developing new medical practices and philosophical ideas. The Omayyad Empire is considered to be a high point of early Islamic civilization.

Under the Omayyads, however, political administration, education, intellectual pursuits, and other aspects of city life were more highly valued than rural life. This caused conflict between the predominantly rural inhabitants of the Middle East and the urban dwellers. That conflict, combined with the strife between Sunni and Shia groups and among clans, finally overwhelmed the Omayyads around the middle of the eighth century. Muslims based in Baghdad, with the support of Shia Muslims, conquered the area but neglected the coastal areas, which fell under the control of Egypt.

THE CRUSADES

During the tenth and eleventh centuries, Syria devolved into many local principalities and emirates, and this political fragmentation allowed invading French Crusaders to take over much of northern and western Syria. The Crusaders came in waves, building mighty hilltop fortresses that still stand. A primary focus of the battle between the Crusaders and the Muslims and Jews was for control of Jerusalem, which was a holy city to all of them.

Despite their success on the coastal plains and in the coastal mountains, however, the Crusaders never had much impact in central and eastern Syria, and the cities of Damascus, Homs, and Hama were never taken.

In 1169, the Syrian sultan Nureddin sent his general Salah al-Din (commonly called Saladin) to the Egyptian royal court. Saladin took control of Egypt in 1171, and after Nureddin's death, he became sultan of both Egypt and Syria. He attacked the Crusaders and forced the European armies out of Jerusalem in 1188.

THE ARRIVAL OF THE OTTOMANS

Approximately three hundred years after the Crusaders were driven out, the Turkish Ottomans took over the land and probably had the strongest influence on modern Syria. They brought a certain amount of material success to the land and were Sunni Muslims like most Syrians. They allowed local administration by Arabs who were at least nominally loyal to them. These Arabs were wealthy landowners with deep roots in cities such as Damascus and Aleppo. The Ottomans ruled for about four hundred years, until the end of World War I.

AN INDEPENDENT SYRIA

After the Turks were driven out of Syria, France and England competed for the spoils. They both had political, religious, and economic reasons for wanting a presence in the area. France finally won control of Syria.

Syria rebelled against French rule from 1925 to 1927 but was crushed by superior military power, including a French bombardment of Damascus.

The Syrians continued unsuccessfully to fight for their independence until Article 78 was adopted by the new United Nations in June 1945. It stated that members of the United Nations could not be placed under occupation by another country. The Arab League declared that the presence of French and British forces in the Levant violated the countries' sovereignty. Finally, after a lot of wrangling and hostilities, French troops left Syria on April 17, 1946. This is called Evacuation Day, which is celebrated as a national holiday.

GROWING PAINS

Syria started its new life as an independent country with enormous problems. In 1947, the United Nations awarded a part of Palestine, which in Ottoman times was part of Greater Syria, to the Zionist Jews of Europe, in opposition to the wishes of the Arab majority in the area and of the neighboring Arab countries. There was almost immediate fighting between Israel and the Arab states, including Syria, which would carry on for decades.

Syria and Egypt were each represented as a green star on the new flag of the United Arab Republic.

Hafez al-Assad

In addition, Syria's economy was weak. Few roads or railroads were built under the French occupation, and the poor land and harsh climate of the new country made self-sufficiency difficult. The lushest, most fertile parts of the Levant now formed the new countries of Lebanon and Israel or had been given to Turkey before World War II. Syria was left with arid lands more suitable for grazing than farming.

The difficulties Syria inherited resulted in a series of military coups from the very beginning of independence. The threat of military takeover continued to plague Syria.

In 1958, Syria and Egypt tried to put Pan-Arabism—the belief that all Arab people should be part of one nation—into action. Pan-Arabism had been an Arab ideal since the early twentieth century. Their effort at confederation, the United Arab Republic, was, however, short-lived. Egypt completely dominated Syria, and the union disintegrated in 1961.

In the mid-1960s, a group of dissident military officers came to power through the growing and powerful Baath Party, a Pan-Arab party in Syria and Iraq. The Baath Party was founded by two schoolteachers from Damascus, one Christian and one Muslim. Inspired by the new spirit of nationalism, the unifying factor was not religious belief but the oppression of Arabs. The Baath Party itself was strongly socialistic, which appealed to the Syrian masses; they were tired of the Sunni aristocrats, who had cooperated with the Ottomans for centuries, enhancing their own wealth and power.

Hafez al-Assad, then minister of defense, organized a bloodless military coup and assumed the Syrian presidency in 1971.

ISIL is a militant terrorist organization, also known as the Islamic State of Iraq and Syria (ISIS) or simply the Islamic State (IS). In June 2014, ISIL declared it had established a caliphate, an Islamic state which follows religious laws ruled a caliph—a descendent of the Prophet Muhammad who rules as the Prophet's representative on Earth with absolute authority.

ISIL was born out of al-Qaeda, the terrorist group responsible for the September 11, 2001, attacks on the Twin Towers. As of March 2015, the Red Cross estimated ten million people were living in regions under ISIL control spanning across Syria and Iraq. The current leader of ISIL is Abu Bakr al-Baghdadi.

The al-Nusra Front is a separate offshoot from al-Qaeda, which also plans to establish a caliphate, although mostly in Syria.

The brutality of both groups has shocked the world with mass killings, suicide bombings, and public beheadings. Much of the international military effort in Syria is focused on defeating these militant jihadists.

THE ASSAD YEARS

Throughout the 1960s and 1970s, Assad ruled Syria with an iron fist. During a 1982 uprising of the Muslim Brotherhood, a fundamentalist Islamic group, Assad massacred twenty thousand people in the central city of Hama. In 1976, Assad's government deployed thousands of Syrian troops into neighboring Lebanon to fight in a civil war that had broken out between Christians and Muslims. The Syrian forces gained control of areas in eastern and northern Lebanon. Despite several attempts by the Lebanese and the international community to remove them, Syrian forces remained in the country until 2005. In 2000, Assad passed away, ending his twenty-nine-year rule. He was succeeded by his son, Bashar.

DAMASCUS SPRING

The early period following Bashar al-Assad's presidency, between mid-2000 and the fall of 2001, became known as the Damascus Spring. Initially, with the younger Assad as the new head of state, there were high hopes of government reform and the chance of democracy for Syria. *Muntadayats*, open forums discussing political and social reform, were held throughout Damascus and other major cities. These reforms were formally presented in September 2000 as the Statement of 99. This petition was signed by ninety-nine Syrian intellectuals and called for the government to end martial law, release all political prisoners, and form laws which would provide basic human rights to Syrians, such as freedom of expression and freedom of assembly. In January 2011, a more aggressive second petition, signed by one thousand intellectuals, once again called for the abolishment of martial law and also demanded a multiparty government system be established.

Initially, the new president and his government appeared ready for changes such as these. Political prisoners were released with the closure of Mezze prison, and six political parties under the National Progressive Front (NPF) opened provincial offices. Human rights organizations were reestablished and did not meet with government opposition. However, in early 2001, the forums were shut down by the Baath government and several

Syrians in Egypt protest to show their support for the growing spirit of revolution in their native country.

of the Damascus Spring leaders were arrested. The hope of reform was quickly lost, and Syria remained under the almost totalitarian rule of Assad and his regime for another ten years.

In March 2011, following uprisings across the Middle East dubbed the Arab Spring, the spirit of revolution awakened in Syria after decades of Baathist rule. The first protests began in the city of Der'a then quickly spread across the country. After several vicious attacks by government forces, peaceful protests by the Syrian people escalated into violence. By 2012, the entire country had descended into civil war, which continues today. Amid the ongoing conflict, the future of Syria remains unknown.

INTERNET LINKS

www.nytimes.com/interactive/2015/09/30/world/middleeast/syria-control-map-isis-rebels-airstrikes.html?_r=0
This interactive map breaks down the movement and occupation of government forces, rebels, the Kurds, and foreign troops in the Syrian civil war.

whc.unesco.org/en/list/20/video
The "Ancient City of Damascus" is a short video highlighting the history of this UNESCO World Heritage site.

www.wsj.com/video/syria-a-brief-history/2D7BB798-53DD-4066-9D88-51DF668464A1.html
This video provides a short overview of Syrian history, leading up to the current civil war.

GOVERNMENT

People opposing the Assad regime stage a protest in Berlin, Germany, on March 15, 2012, the one-year anniversary of the Der'a uprising.

3

• • • • • • • • • • • •
The ancient city of
Damascus is the
capital of Syria,
officially called the
Syrian Arab Republic.

SINCE GAINING INDEPENDENCE IN 1946, Syria has struggled to find political stability in the wake of long-term authoritarian rule. Today, the crumbling Baathist government is fighting to maintain control of strategic areas under the leadership of President Bashar al-Assad. Amid the fighting, a complex web of shifting political interests and alliances—both within the country and internationally—has formed. Among these conflicting groups, many are trying to work toward a resolution to bring peace and democracy to Syria in the coming years.

GOVERNMENT STRUCTURE

In 1971, Hafez al-Assad ("al-Assad" means "the lion" in Arabic) was elected Syria's president by an assembly of his own choosing. The 1973 constitution gave the president almost total control of the country.

The Syrian president is head of state. The prime minister, appointed by the president, serves as head of the government. The president also appoints a cabinet of ministers of varying size. In addition, there is a

Mohammad Jihad al-Laham, the leader of the People's Council.

People's Council of 250 seats. Elections are held every four years with the last held in 2012 and the next scheduled for 2016. All Syrians over the age of eighteen can vote and elect councilors. A number of seats are reserved for farmers and workers. Women are guaranteed equality in elections and currently hold thirty seats in the People's Council.

The People's Council proposes laws, debates cabinet programs, and approves the national budget. The council can override presidential vetoes by a two-thirds majority but has never done so. Although the constitution requires that the president be a Muslim, there are no religious qualifications for the assembly. At the regional level, Syria is divided into fourteen *muhafazats*, or provinces, overseen by a governor.

Presidential elections are held every seven years. When President Hafez al-Assad died in 2000, the Baath Party nominated his son, Bashar, as its new presidential candidate. In the following election, Bashar ran uncontested and was duly elected with 97.29 percent of the vote. The most recent election was held in June 2014. For the first time in over forty years, multiple candidates were listed on the ballot: Assad and two independent candidates. However, with an Assad victory of 88.7 percent, many have called the election a sham against the backdrop of civil unrest. As noted by US secretary of state John Kerry: "You can't have an election where millions of your millions don't even have an ability to vote."

THE BAATH PARTY

In Arabic, *baath* means "resurrection" or "renaissance" and refers to the party's origin as a movement in support of Arab unity and nationalism. The party, which operates under the slogan "unity, freedom, socialism," was founded after World War II and gained strength when Palestinian lands were given to European Jews to form Israel. Baathists felt that the lack of Arab unity had made this possible.

BASHAR AL-ASSAD

Born in 1965, Bashar al-Assad is the second son of former Syrian president Hafez al-Assad. He lived largely out of the public eye for many years, first attending university in Damascus to become an ophthalmologist, then later traveling to London to further his studies. Following the sudden death of his brother in 1994, who had been the intended heir of Hafez, Bashar was called home to be groomed as  *the successor to the Baath leadership. Under his father's direction, Bashar trained in the military, rising to the rank of colonel, and also headed a campaign weeding out corruption in the government.*

When Bashar assumed the presidency following his father's death in 2000, many Syrians hoped he would lead his people into the twenty-first century by bringing democratic and economic reforms to the country. These hopes were dashed after only a few short years. Under Bashar's command, the 2011 anti-government protests staged across Syria met with unprecedented violence. These actions, coupled with a refusal to bring about political change, added fuel to the uprisings that propelled the country toward civil war.

The 1973 constitution established the Baath Party as the "leading party of the state and society," an article that was removed from the new constitution issued in 2012. The party currently dominates the alliance of ten political parties known as the National Progressive Front (NPF) that controls Syrian politics. While other parties exist, Baathists effectively control the government, most media, and what remains of Syria's military.

THE JUDICIAL BRANCH

Syria's system of justice is based on the French model. There are civil and criminal courts. Lawsuits and other civil cases often take years to settle.

"With our souls, with our blood, we sacrifice for you, Bashar!" is a common pro-Assad chant heard from supporters of the Baathist government.

A Sharia judge listens to a case.

The State Security Court, dissolved in 2011 by Assad, once tried political opponents the government accused of being "security risks." Trials in this system violated most international standards for fair trials.

Courts governing personal status, like birth, marriage, and inheritance, are divided according to religion. For Muslims, there is a court that follows the Muslim code, called the Sharia. There are separate courts for Druze, Roman Catholics, Orthodox believers, Protestants, and Jews.

ARMED FORCES

Syria is widely regarded as a country with serious human rights problems. Hafez al-Assad was known to use arbitrary imprisonment and torture to suppress opposition to his rule. Initially after becoming president in 2000, Bashar started to relinquish control and periodically released political prisoners as a gesture of tolerance to those who opposed the government. These concessions, however, were short-lived and quickly dissolved back to the familiar authoritarian rule of the past.

The Syrian Armed Forces are divided into the army, navy, and air force, with the police and security forces maintaining domestic control. The country maintains a large armed force in part because it has been at war on and off with Israel for decades and in part because it has had to use force to suppress dissident movements within Syria.

Military service lasting eighteen months is compulsory for men between eighteen and forty years of age. Service can be waived for those with medical conditions or who are studying at university. Women are not required to serve; however, they are able to voluntarily join.

Since the war started, the Syrian government has increased its enforcement of the mandatory service. In Damascus and other cities, men have been arrested and forced to enlist in the military. At security checkpoints, they are subjected to additional screening to determine whether they have

INTERNATIONAL INVOLVEMENT

The international community has come under heavy criticism for its late intervention in the Syrian crisis. Since 2014, many of the world's superpowers have been drawn into the conflict from all sides, particularly with the growing threat of ISIL and its attacks on foreign soil.

While the United States has been reluctant to take an active military role on the ground in Syria following the recent war in Iraq, the government has provided training to opposition forces fighting within Syria. In the fall of 2014, a US-led coalition began airstrikes against ISIL and other terrorist affiliates in Syria. Many nations are active in the airstrikes, and the coalition has the support of dozens more. After the ISIL attack in Paris in November 2015, France and several other countries increased their commitment to fighting terror in Syria. On the political front, the United States supports the Syrian National Coalition and is calling for the end of Baathist rule in Syria, to be replaced by a transitional government.

Much of the Middle East is actively participating in the US-led coalition. Syria's northern neighbor, Turkey, has advocated for the removal of Assad since 2011 and has absorbed nearly two million refugees since the war began. Although critical of the West's late entry into the conflict, as the fighting and humanitarian crisis has worsened, Turkey has begun actively working as part of the coalition, with air bases in Turkey serving as the launch sites for airstrikes. The Gulf states (Saudi Arabia, Bahrain, Kuwait, Qatar, Oman, and the United Arab Emirates) are also involved in the coalition.

In support of pro-government forces, Iran and Russia are Assad's strongest allies. As a permanent member of the UN Security Council, Russia has blocked international attempts that may have removed Assad from power, with the aid of China. The Putin-led government supplies weapons to the Syrian government and has important military installments located within the country, including an air base in Latakia and a naval base on the Mediterranean. In September 2015, Russia began airstrikes, claiming ISIL and terrorists as its target. However, evidence suggests the contrary: that Russia has also been targeting groups that oppose the Assad regime and Russian interests in Syria. Iran is similarly supplying weapons and pouring billions of dollars into Syria to support Assad.

Despite their conflicting interests, all international parties have expressed desire to move toward a peaceful solution for Syria. However, as the fighting rages on and more parties are drawn into the conflict, the road to peace grows only more complex.

fulfilled their service requirements. To avoid being forced into the chaotic fighting, many young men have fled the country.

The Free Syrian Army (FSA), formed in August 2011, is the largest force fighting against the Assad regime. The FSA is largely composed of fighters who once served in the Syrian Armed Forces and is loosely made up of small groups fighting in various parts of the country.

OPPOSITION OF THE GOVERNMENT

Syrians have a strong libertarian streak and are wary of any government. Particularly in rural areas, people generally believe that the government does not understand their problems. In urban areas, regional jealousies fostered tensions with the government, leading to the 2011 uprisings. Many Syrians feel that the Baathist government favors the minority Alawites, the Islamic sect to which the Assad family and many of the government's senior officials belong.

The people who support the government are those who have benefited socially, politically, or financially or who feel that a secular government

Many women have enlisted in the Syrian military to support the Assad government.

protects the diverse religious practices in Syria better than one that imposes religious beliefs as law.

Presently, there is a resounding call from many Syrians and members of the international community for the resignation of Assad. For many groups, this is a nonnegotiable condition they insist be met before any peace talks take place.

The National Coalition of Syrian Revolution and Opposition Forces is the leading political organization against Syria's current government and is recognized internationally by over one hundred countries as the legitimate representation of Syria's people. The coalition, founded in November 2012, has representation from many Syrian minorities. The group's headquarters are located outside of Syria in Cairo, Egypt. The organization has operated under leader Khaled Khoja since January 2015. The coalition is backed by Western powers and supports the Free Syrian Army as its military branch within Syria. In December 2015, the coalition was among sixty-five delegates invited to a conference in Saudi Arabia to implement the Geneva Communique, a roadmap to Syrian peace assembled by major world powers in 2012.

Rivalry among the country's various religious and ethnic minorities has been an ongoing source of instability in Syria. National loyalty traditionally takes second place to religious and ethnic loyalties, so the government appears at times to Syrians to represent no more than another faction among factions.

INTERNET LINKS

www.bbc.com/news/10338256
This BBC article provides a background on the recent political situation in Syria and includes biographical information on President Bashar al-Assad.

en.etilaf.org
The official website of the National Coalition of Syrian Revolution and Opposition Forces.

www.understandingwar.org/sites/default/files/Backgrounder_ SyriasPoliticalStruggle_Spring2012.pdf
This article from the Institute for the Study of War explains the Syrian political scene following the 2012 election.

ECONOMY

In early 2016, a 200-pound Syrian banknote was worth less than $1 US.

4

THE WAR HAS WREAKED HAVOC ON the Syrian economy; it is difficult to measure the true cost of the conflict. An estimated four out of five Syrians are living in poverty and the humanitarian crisis fueled by the fighting has placed a huge strain on the country's fractured infrastructure. Further adding to this crisis, international sanctions have limited the import and export markets available to supply Syrians internally and provide for the sale of goods and services produced within the country.

Since the war began, the value of the Syrian currency, the pound, has plummeted by approximately 80 percent.

FROM THE LAND

In the 1970s, 50 percent of the population was involved in farming; today only 17 percent of Syria's labor force work in this sector. Agriculture contributes about 18.1 percent of the gross domestic product (GDP). Wheat, barley, cotton, legumes like chickpeas and lentils, fruit, vegetables, and sheep are the mainstays of farming.

Before more recent times, Syria was nearly self-sufficient in basic food products. It produced a large amount of chicken and lamb, and some beef. Its primary vegetables and fruits were chickpeas, lentils,

A farmer tills a field in Der'a, once part of the nation's breadbasket.

olives, and sugar beets. Syria had also become the world's fourth-largest producer of olive oil. In 2015, early forecasts projected a total of 236,997 tons (215,000 metric tons) of oil to be produced in the country, an increase of 105 percent from the 2014 crop.

The southwestern corner of the country was once the nation's breadbasket, supplying enough grains to meet Syrian needs as well as some surplus for export. However, with much farmland and agricultural supplies lost to fighting, in 2014 Syria imported approximately 1.65 million tons (1.5 million t) of wheat. In the summer of 2015, a UN report stated that nearly ten million Syrians were "food insecure."

FROM THE EARTH

The war has wreaked havoc on Syria's industrial sector, resulting in a decline in production in 2014. The energy and manufacturing industries have been the most affected by the conflict, with important oil fields and the city of Aleppo, once the country's economic capital, falling under rebel control. While crude oil exports alone accounted for $5 billion US in revenue in 2010, by 2014, Syria's total exports across all sectors only generated approximately $3 billion US. The textile industry, also once an important part of Syria's economy, accounted for 63 percent of the industrial sector before. Exports of yarn, fabric, and clothing brought in about $3.3 billion US. Many factories have been damaged in the conflict. Today, only 10 percent of Syria's textile factories are operating and producing goods. The UN has estimated that it may take thirty years for the Syrian economy to recover to its pre-war GDP growth rate of 5 percent (2010).

FROM HOME AND ABROAD

Syria's primary exports are oil, cotton (grown mostly around the Euphrates River), vegetables, fruit, and textiles. There are also a growing number of import-export businesses that export such things as food and industrial

In the Middle East, oil is the backbone of most countries' economies. In Syria, oil was first discovered in 1956. Although many foreign countries have ceased operations in Syria during the conflict, the country is currently ranked twenty-seventh in global oil production. Most of the oil is concentrated near the Iraqi border and in small pockets throughout the country. This commodity is transported in and out of Syria through the ports of Baniyas, Tartus, and Latakia.

ISIL presently controls approximately 80 percent of the country's oil production, with the production of ninety thousand barrels per day. The Assad regime controls 8 percent, with the remaining 12 percent held by Kurdish fighters. Much of the oil controlled by ISIL is sold to the Syrian government and abroad on the black market.

products. The main imports are machinery and transportation equipment, electrical generation equipment, food, livestock, metal products, chemicals, plastics, yarn, and paper.

In 2015, more than twelve million Syrians were unemployed.

REVIVING THE ECONOMY

From the coup in the mid-1960s up to the mid-1980s, Syria's economy was highly centralized. All utilities, transportation, and heavy industry were owned and operated by the government. Small merchants and craft workers, professional people, farmers, and shepherds were free to operate their own means of livelihood, but with price controls.

About the time the Soviet Union—a long-time patron of Syria—began to look for ways to decentralize economic control, so did Syria. Investment Law 10, a 1991 directive issued by the president, liberalized economic restrictions

THE COST OF LIVING

For many Syrians, with food prices skyrocketing, it is becoming increasingly difficult to cover the basic cost of providing food for their families. Some staples such as bread were subsidized by the government to a cost of only 2 Syrian pounds (SYP) for a flat, round loaf. However, as of February 2015, prices increased, making it more difficult for families to afford a loaf of bread. Plus, there is only a limited quantity available. In some areas, the cost of bread produced by private bakeries has risen by 500 percent.

In April 2015, one man living in Damascus reported on the average cost of living compared to what many Syrians earn as a salary. The average salary in the capital was about 15,000 SYP, the equivalent of $50 in US currency. To buy basic foodstuffs, Syrians in Damascus at this time paid:

- *1,000 SYP for 2.2 pounds (1 kilogram) of bananas*
- *3,000 SYP for 2.2. pounds (1 kg) of beef*
- *300 SYP for 2.2 pounds (1 kg) of tomatoes*
- *800 SYP for thirty eggs*

and encouraged private investment in certain commercial and industrial areas. The government, however, remains the country's utilities manager. It heavily subsidizes public transportation, sets prices on fuel and basic foods, and operates most heavy industries.

Assad promised reforms and privatization in the economy. A few small changes were made, such as allowing private banks to open and reducing some subsidies on food to help farmers earn their livings.

INTERNATIONAL SANCTIONS

For decades, Syria has been subject to economic sanctions, particularly from the United States, for its leniency toward terrorist groups in the Middle East. Since 2011, the sanctions imposed by the international community have greatly increased. In August 2011, US president Barack Obama signed an order freezing all assets of the Syrian government, banning the import of any oil from Syria, and prohibiting any Americans from conducting business with the Syrian government. In 2013, these sanctions were amended, allowing for Syrians in areas controlled by the opposition to import US goods for agriculture, infrastructure, and oil production.

The European Union has imposed similar sanctions, also making concessions to support the opposition. An arms embargo, instituted in May 2011, was partially lifted in May 2013 to allow some European countries to supply Syrian opposition forces with military equipment for their internal conflict.

INTERNET LINKS

www.chathamhouse.org/publication/syrias-economy-administrative-institutions

An analysis of the crumbling Syrian economy since the start of the 2011 conflict.

country.eiu.com/syria

The *Economist* Intelligence Unit provides a current analysis of the Syrian economy and future projections.

www.syrianef.org/En/interactive-map

The Syrian Economic Forum supplies an interactive map that shows the fluctuating price of goods in Syria's main cities.

ENVIRONMENT

The Barada River all but disappears during the scorching summer months.

5

H ISTORICALLY, THE GOVERNMENT has had few policies and ministries focusing on protecting the fragile Syrian landscape and the wildlife that lives within it. This has resulted in high levels of pollution in Syria's urban centers and waterways. In the mid-2000s, the government started to take a more active role in safeguarding these resources, but with the ongoing crisis in Syria, environmental concerns have taken a backseat to more pressing humanitarian concerns.

CITY POLLUTION

Air pollution is a large issue in Syria, particularly in its urban centers. Idling vehicles greatly contribute to this problem. In the mid-2000s, on Damascus roads, vehicles traveled at an average speed of only 1.8 to 3.1 miles per hour (3—5 kmh). Many of these vehicles, mostly buses, run on diesel fuel, which is not a renewable energy source and contributes to climate change. Additionally, during the winter months, many Syrians heat their homes using diesel heaters, which also pollute the air.

Buses idle on the streets of Damascus.

Air pollution has not been monitored in great detail in Syria; however, studies conducted in Damascus and other major cities have recommended that the country move toward green, renewable sources of energy. Small steps were made toward this goal before the war. Electric scooters have grown in popularity in some cities; in 2009, Damascus University constructed a prototype for an electric car that used solar panels and could travel up to 37 miles per hour (60 kmh), and in 2010, the government introduced some "green diesel" pumps, which had a lesser impact on the environment.

Oil refineries and processing plants in cities like Homs, Banias, and Damascus also add to the air pollution problem. As Syria industrialized, no restrictions were placed on the location of heavy industry. Therefore, much of it is found in residential and office areas. Heavy industry is not regulated, so oil refineries, petrochemical and cement producers, and other such plants pump their waste into the cities' water sources, causing water pollution. They also emit toxic fumes and bury solid waste in open spaces.

SALT IN THE SOIL

Syria has long depended on irrigation to grow crops. However, if water is not drained away from the surface efficiently, mineral salts in the soil dissolve in the water. When the water evaporates, the salts are left on the surface of the soil, and the soil becomes salinized. Very few plants will grow in salinized soil.

The area around Aleppo was converted to cotton production in the 1950s after large-scale diesel-fueled irrigation systems were built there. By the 1960s, a lot of land was too salt laden to produce any crops and had to be abandoned. Using deeper drainage systems, some of this land is being brought back into cultivation. After washing the land, barley can be grown for a few years before other crops are introduced.

EXPLOITING SYRIA'S WATERWAYS

In much of the Middle East, water is a highly prized commodity. Syria, Turkey, and Iraq have the most dependence on the Euphrates River, while Kuwait, Saudi Arabia, and Jordan also rely on its life-giving power in the arid desert. Syria in particular relies on this waterway for 50 percent of its freshwater, with some cities such as Aleppo and its southern neighbor Salamiyah sourcing 100 percent of their freshwater from the Euphrates.

In recent years, environmental dangers have threatened the sustainability of many waterways in the Middle East. Water has been overexploited for agricultural and hydroelectric use, pollution has not been regulated, and population growth has placed added strain on the flow of water. In the past fifty years, thirty-two dams and man-made barriers have been constructed along the Euphrates's course, lessening the water quality and reducing its flow by 40 to 45 percent since the 1970s. The Syrian crisis has added to these concerns, with key infrastructure such as dams falling under control of militant groups such as ISIL and fractured relations between the many nations reliant on the river. ISIL has gained control of three dams: the Tishreen Dam near Aleppo, and the Tabqa and Baath Dams, located farther downstream. All three are crucial to regulating the flow of water in the Euphrates.

In light of these concerns, and the increased effects of climate change, sustainable management of these waterways is direly needed. It will be essential for the countries that utilize these resources to form a partnership to sustainably develop its use; what affects one country will ultimately affect another. If the rivers continue to be overtaxed, the effect will be disastrous.

PRESERVING THE STEPPE

A shepherd grazes his sheep outside the ruins of Palmyra.

The eastern part of the country, called the steppe, or Badia, is used mostly by nomadic and seminomadic sheepherders. The main environmental problem in this region is the loss of soil to wind erosion. Even light winds can carry sand and dirt away if the land is not protected by plant cover. The main causes of this problem are overgrazing and the use of heavy trucks for transportation of water, food, and animals.

Herders move their animals around according to seasonal rainfall and plant growth patterns. Traditionally, arid zones such as the Syrian steppe were not harmed by this, but changes in the last half-century have taken their toll. In 1950, there were about 2.6 million sheep grazing in the steppe; by 2010, there were an estimated 15.5 million—nearly six times more. Shepherds were able to increase their flocks because the government subsidized feed for the animals and did not enforce restrictions on when and for how long different areas could be grazed. As a result, the steppe suffered from overgrazing. Since the war, however, Syria's sheep population has dropped by about 30 percent to under 12 million head. With fewer animals grazing, this may give the fragile steppe a much-needed opportunity for regrowth.

Additionally, herders have traditionally used certain types of bushes and shrubs for fuel and medicine for millennia, but as their population increased, this practice started to have a negative impact on the environment. The traditional practice of uprooting plants rather than harvesting branches meant that the soil was exposed to the force of wind erosion. In the same way, large vehicles chew up the crusty layer on top of the soil, exposing the earth beneath to erosion.

The Syrian government, together with the United Nations Food and Agriculture Organization (FAO) and the Italian government, initiated the

The northern bald ibis was believed to be extinct in Syria and most of the Mediterranean region. The last sightings in Syria were in 1928 and the last wild breeding colony died out in Turkey in 1989. The only known populations of these birds were those raised in captivity in Turkey and a few hundred wild animals living in Morocco.

Then, in 2002, Gianluca Serra, an Italian working with the Al Talila project, heard rumors from local hunters and herders that birds matching the ibis's description had been sighted near the ancient city of Palmyra in central Syria. Using a questionnaire and photos of ibises and related species, Serra and his Syrian colleagues began a systematic survey of the region. After two years, they finally found the nesting site of three pairs and a seventh adult bird.

The northern bald ibis is a migratory bird that needs wild or semi-wild areas where it can find its favorite foods of insects, young frogs, and snakes while it nests and raises its young. Humans disrupt this habitat when they farm or draw too much water from rainy-season ponds, destroying the breeding grounds of the ibis's prey.

Sadly, however, for the northern ibis of Palmyra, their presence has not been seen since 2014. Many people think the ibis's disappearance is attributed to aggravations by violence and ecological damage in Palmyra, however, the northern ibis's territory was in decline before such conflicts had escalated. In May 2015, Serra speculated all of the known northern ibis had died, ending the existence of the species in Syria.

Rangeland Rehabilitation and Establishment of a Wildlife Refuge Project in 1996. The project reseeded a few hundred acres of steppe with native plants and established an education center for visitors and locals to learn more about steppe conservation. The highlight of the project was the establishment of the Al Talila Reserve about 18.6 miles (30 km) east of Palmyra.

FRESH WATER, ANCIENT WELLS

The United Nations Development Program (UNDP) has been working in Syria toward its Millennium Goals, one of which is environmental sustainability. With much of Syria's infrastructure in ruins, many people in rural communities do not have access to clean water.

Under the leadership of the UNDP, thirty-six ancient Roman wells were recycled in 2013 for use by local farmers. These two-thousand-year-old wells were drained and enlarged to collect water from rain showers and surface aquifers. The wells support 450 families, allowing many Syrians to provide food for their families and grow produce to sell at the market. The project also provided work and a much-needed sense of community.

Since 2011, levels of nitrous dioxide, a greenhouse gas, over Damascus have dropped by over 50 percent, which is attributed to the vast number of people leaving the country.

PROTECTING SYRIA'S DIVERSITY

Syria's first wildlife refuge, Al Talila, officially opened in 2003. It is small, with 2,470 acres (1,000 hectares) of land, but its significance is enormous. By fencing off the reserve from grazing domestic animals, this area shows how productive well-maintained land can be. Endangered Arabian oryx and gazelles were imported from Saudi Arabia to repopulate the land. In just a few years, their numbers increased from eight to thirteen oryx and thirty to fifty-three gazelles.

For years, biologists have been able to study steppe ecology in the reserve, and they trained local Bedouins, who make their homes in Al Talila, as nature guides. New species of animals have been discovered there, such as a new species of beetle (*Aphodaulacus talilensis*), named after the reserve. Al Talila stands as a symbol for Syrians of what their country once was and could be again with careful management of human and natural needs. It has also served as an example of how to successfully integrate desert communities within protected areas, particularly for the nearby country of Jordan.

A THIRST FOR CHANGE

In recent years, some experts have attributed climate change, and the Syrian government's lack of management in light of these changes, as a contributing factor to the civil war. A severe drought plagued the Middle East between 2006 and 2009 and devastated the country's agricultural sector, killing many livestock and resulting in low crop yields. Many Syrians who had previously spent their lives farming the land found themselves without an income. This created a movement of about 1.5 million people toward urban centers. While the drought certainly was not the primary catalyst behind the war, it was a contributing factor to the arrival of many disheartened Syrians in the country's major cities.

A herd of oryx.

INTERNET LINKS

www.birdlife.org/datazone/speciesfactsheet.php?id=3791
Learn all about the northern bald ibis.

www.insightonconflict.org/2014/07/toxic-footprint-syrias-war
This article speculates on some of the long-term environmental effects of the war.

www.sy.undp.org/content/syria/en/home/mdgoverview/overview/mdg7
Read about some of the projects the UNDP has undertaken in Syria to work toward environmental stability.

SYRIANS

A stream of Syrian Kurds flees across the border to Turkey.

6

More than four million people have fled the country since 2011. Millions more are displaced within the country, seeking refuge from the fighting and threat of ISIL.

SYRIANS TODAY ARE AN amalgamation of the country's past, with most people having descended from Phoenicians, Babylonians, and Assyrians. Today, these people are all known as Arabs. Before the war began, 56 percent of Syrians lived in urban centers, namely the major cities of Damascus, Homs, Aleppo, and Hama. That number has decreased as people leave their homeland for other areas abroad.

BY THE NUMBERS

Most Syrians are young; almost 33 percent of the population is fourteen years of age or younger, while less than 10 percent are over fifty-five. The population grew rapidly in the last century. At the end of World War I, there were 200,000 Syrians; in 1972, there were 4.5 million; by 1986, 12 million; and by 2011, 21.96 million. Since then, with a constant flow of people leaving the country, it is hard to measure the country's population. In July 2014, it was estimated at 17,064,854.

Family sizes have also shrunk over the past several decades. In the 1960s, the average family included eight children. In 2015, the average mother had between two to three kids.

A DIVIDED SOCIETY

In Syria, the lighter-skinned people usually dominate the top socioeconomic positions and the darker-skinned people the bottom ones. Top government officials, business owners, and models in television commercials are almost uniformly lighter skinned and often European in appearance, whereas construction workers, janitors, garbage haulers, and street cleaners are predominantly darker skinned.

A MOSAIC OF CULTURES

Arabs live in all parts of the country; non-Arab groups generally live in partial isolation from one another, either in their own village or cluster of villages, or in specific quarters of towns and cities.

KURDS The Kurds are believed to constitute about 9 percent of the population. Most live in the foothills of the Taurus Mountains north of Aleppo, in Al-Jazirah, near Jarabulus northeast of Aleppo, or in the Quarter of the Kurds on the outskirts of Damascus. They are a fiercely independent people with a deep pride in their history and traditions. Many arrived from Turkey between 1924 and 1938, in reaction to the Turkish attempt to suppress Kurdish culture by banning their language.

Kurds now live in the mountain regions of Turkey, Iraq, Iran, and Syria. Since the early part of this century, Kurds have been fighting for the independence of this region, which they call Kurdistan. Kurds are traditionally nomadic herders, and they speak Kurdish, an Indo-European language. They are mostly Sunni Muslims.

Young Syrian girls study at a school for refugees in Turkey.

Syrian society includes a variety of social groups of various sizes that lack any set of shared values and loyalties that might bind the population into one nation. Differences in language, region, religion, ethnicity, and way of life produce a large number of separate communities, each with a strong internal loyalty and solidarity. One observer has spoken of the "empty center" of Syrian society, the lack of an influential group embodying a national consensus.

One reason for this fragmentation is the historical isolation of different groups. Christian groups have always played a prominent role in Syria, especially in the west and north. When the Omayyads first arrived, the various Christian groups, perhaps fearing persecution, moved farther into the mountains, forming separate communities. In later years, minority sects of Islam did the same. Under Egyptian rule, non-Muslim groups were given some autonomy. Under the Ottomans, the practice spread, creating what was called the Millet system, which gave Jewish and Christian communities their own governments within the empire.

Religious distinctions are psychologically and politically the most significant ones. Loyalty to one's religious group, rather than to the Syrian nation, is an important value. The religious communities are largely self-contained social systems that regulate much of the daily life of their members and receive their primary loyalty.

In addition, language differences and differences in social organization between villagers, Bedouins, and city dwellers further fragment the society. Each of these groups practices a distinct, usually hereditary, way of life. Syria's post-independence history is largely the story of conflict between minority groups and the central government, which climaxed in the spring of 2011.

Kurdish women do not wear the veil and enjoy considerable freedom, working and interacting socially with men. However, they are not encouraged to participate in political activities. In the villages, women prepare food and clothing and bring water to the house. Men build the houses and take care of the animals. All help with the planting.

Dress varies for Kurdish women. Traditional dress for men includes baggy pants bound at the ankles and worn with a tunic, vest, and cummerbund.

Young Syrian Kurds dressed in Western-style fashions.

They wear a brightly colored turban or yellow fur cap, and traditionally carry a curved dagger and rifle. Most Kurds, however, now wear European-style clothing, although their traditional dress remains a symbol of Kurdish unity, as does their appearance of fierceness. Kurds, too, have been drawn into the war, fighting ISIL and other rebel groups in the mountainous region between Syria and Turkey.

ARMENIANS Most of the Armenians in Syria arrived as refugees from Turkey between 1925 and 1945. They are city or town dwellers, with more than 60 percent living in Aleppo. Other large populations live in the cities of Kessab, Qamishli, Yacubiyah, Kobane, and the Quarter of the Armenians in Damascus.

Many villagers in northwestern Syria are of Armenian descent. Armenians belong to the Armenian Orthodox Church or the Armenian Catholic Church. Their language is Armenian, an Indo-European language. They work chiefly in trade, small industry, or crafts and have a strong economic position, especially in Aleppo. They are the largest unassimilated group and retain many of their own customs, maintain their own schools, and read Armenian newspapers.

Before 2011, there was an estimated one hundred thousand Armenians living in Syria; as of August 2015, fifteen thousand have fled back to Armenia.

TURKS AND OTHER GROUPS The Turks are seminomadic herders in Al-Jazirah and along the Euphrates River, and farmers in the Aleppo area. Most have assimilated into Arab culture, but some still speak Turkish and retain ethnic traditions. There are also small numbers of Circassians (descendants of Muslim nomads from the Caucasus), Assyrians, and Jews.

BEHIND THE VEIL

Despite its large Muslim population. Syria has always prided itself on being a secular nation, with its government not tied to any single religion. While wearing a hijab is common among Syrian Muslims, the Syrian government viewed the niqab, a veil which fully covers the face except for the eyes, as a side of hardline Islamism. In 2010, the government took a firm position on the niqab, banning women who dressed in these veils from attending and working at universities. They also relocated 1,200 teachers who dressed in the niqab from primary and secondary schools. Many secular Syrians supported the ban, including women's rights groups. However, the ban was short-lived, lasting for only one year as the government came under pressure from its many Muslim citizens to allow the niqab in educational facilities.

Presently, in areas controlled by ISIL and other Islamic extremists, many women have come under attack for not following traditional Muslim dress codes, such as wearing a hijab or niqab. Many are being forced to follow fundamental Islam in fear of violent repercussions.

CLOTHING

It would be hard to find more diversity in dress anywhere else than in Syria. With such a large blend of cultures—every sect of Islam, both Eastern and Western Christianity, and disparate tribes from one corner of the country to the other—the clothing is often a treat for the eyes. A young woman wearing a white scarf and a raincoat (even in the burning heat of summer) can be seen arm-in-arm with her best friend—another young woman in tight blue jeans, with teased hair, heavy makeup, and loads of jewelry. A father in kaftan (a man's gown) and kaffiyeh (ku-FEE-yea), a wrapped cotton headdress, might be walking along with his sons, who are in blue jeans and T-shirts with English words printed on the front. An older woman, draped in black from head to foot, might be with her granddaughter, who is wearing a colorful Syrian dress and earrings that look like small chandeliers. Many wealthy and educated Syrians dress similarly to Europeans or Americans. To add to this mix, every village and tribe of Bedouins has its own particular patterns, hand-embroidered designs, styles, and colors of clothing.

One item that symbolizes not only Middle Eastern dress but Muslim dress in general is the head wrap, also called a hijab. In Syria, there is an endless variety of materials, colors, textures, patterns, and styles of wrapping for both men and women.

A family of Bedouin.

Since 2011, more than 13.5 million Syrians, more than half of whom are children, have fled from their homes. This has created a massive surge of about 4 million refugees, living mostly in the neighboring countries of Turkey, Lebanon, and Jordan.

As of October 2015, UNICEF reported the following breakdown of registered refugees in nearby countries:

Turkey: 1,075,637

Lebanon: 573,315

Egypt: 55,541

Jordan: 327,373

Iraq: 101,976

Other: 13,707

Young Syrians tend to be well dressed and wear Western-style clothing. Particularly in the cities, women wear makeup, jewelry, and high heels. While Western fashions are commonplace, Syrian culture is quite conservative. Some things rarely seen in Syria are bare legs above the calves, bare shoulders or upper arms, shorts on adults (men or women), mini-skirts, short hair on women and girls, and long hair or earrings on men.

INTERNET LINKS

mondoweiss.net/2015/09/refugee-crisis-since
This website presents a comprehensive breakdown of the Syrian refugee crisis.

www.washingtonpost.com/news/worldviews/wp/2013/08/27/the-one-map-that-shows-why-syria-is-so-complicated
This *Washington Post* article highlights the complexities of Syria's diverse ethnic composition.

LIFESTYLE

Coffeehouses are popular meeting spots in the Syrian capital of Damascus. Many men traditionally enjoy puffing on a water pipe while visiting with family and friends.

7

N MOST RURAL AREAS, SYRIANS HAVE retained their traditional ways of life for decades. In the bustling cities, Syrians are very sociable, spending much of their time sitting in coffeehouses or outdoor cafés, visiting with family and friends.

TRAITS OF A SYRIAN

Syrians as a people are extremely social and hospitable. Theirs is a culture that strongly believes in fate, and that belief is reflected in the constant use of the expression *insha'Allah* (in-SHAH-al-LAH), meaning "God willing," whenever they talk about the future. It shows up in various other ways as well. They have a fatalistic sense of humor that is apparent in their political jokes. They do not monitor time and schedules. Being on time does not matter to them because whatever is going to happen is going to happen anyway!

MEETING AND GREETING

Syrians put tons of energy into personal relationships. It is obvious on the streets and in homes, schools, and offices. When Syrian friends greet each other, their hellos and goodbyes seem endless. They ask about each other's families, work, school, and health, and "Where are you going?" or "Can you come have tea or ice cream with us?" Then they say goodbye in several ways and bestow blessings on each other. When they learn English, these habits come through in the new language, and they ask strangers how they are two or three times in a row.

Two men link arms walking past the famous waterwheels of Hama.

Along with social intensity comes physical closeness: male friends walk down the street arm-in-arm or holding hands; men hug and kiss other men, sometimes even on the lips; and women do the same with one another. Syrian friends touch each other constantly. Even engaged lovers and older married people often walk arm-in-arm or hand-in-hand, although this is not as common as physical contact between the same gender.

BLENDING IN

Syrians do not like to stand out from the crowd. Clannishness is part of their tradition: immediate family first, then clan or village (sometimes these are about the same), religion next, then nationality. The variety in dress is part of this group thinking—they dress as their group dresses.

There is little variety in the naming of children. The most common first name for men is Muhammad. Many Muhammads use their middle names for at least a little distinction. Other common men's names are Ahmad, Khalil, Khaled, Yassar, Imad, Samer, or one of a half dozen other widely used names. There is a slightly larger variety of women's names.

FAMILY FIRST

Families are the absolute center of life in Syria, and this shows in many ways. People here cannot understand children leaving home in their late teens or early twenties (unless, of course, they get married), and they often make clear their belief that they are better parents than most Westerners—particularly North Americans. They point to things such as drug use, teenage pregnancy and suicide, and street kids as evidence that this is so. Most young people cannot imagine leaving their parents' homes when they are teenagers. Although some of them complain about family pressures and the lack of privacy, they generally think it is for the well-being of everyone. The idea of putting their aging parents in a nursing home is unacceptable to them (there are no nursing homes in Syria). Although some children are punished harshly at times, children and parents display a lot of affection toward each other.

Meals mark an important time for families to gather and share food and conversation.

Getting married and having children is the top priority for most Syrians. Children are so important (especially sons) that fathers and mothers traditionally use a different name after the first son is born. If they name the son Yassar, the father becomes Abu Yassar—literally "father of Yassar"—and the mother often becomes Umm Yassar—"mother of Yassar." If no sons are born, the mother usually identifies herself as the mother of the firstborn daughter; fathers, however, rarely do this.

THE STRENGTH OF THE CLAN

Clannish behavior in the Arab world developed from the harsh life of the Bedouins. A hostile environment that required vast areas to support a small amount of life led to the need for a strong sense of survival. An individual alone was vulnerable to both the environment and other individuals or groups.

Therefore, the tightest-knit kinship groups thrived the best. A man might feud with his cousin or other relative, but when family members were faced with any threat from outside (even if only perceived), absolute unity was necessary.

Although most Arabs settled down as peasants and cultivators many centuries ago, massive urbanization only took place within the past century.

For thousands of years, the "law of the desert" and clan systems ruled, thus the concept of allegiance to an extended family group became second nature.

This clan loyalty heavily influences modern Arab politics, and who you are related to can be as important as wealth, intelligence, and ability.

THE UNION OF MARRIAGE

Arranged marriages are still very common in Syria, particularly among villagers and Bedouins. Even more modern city people often cannot choose who they marry; if they want a particular mate, both families usually have to agree on the arrangement. First cousins are still a preferred match. Among more modern Syrians, the father of a young woman may approach a young man he would like to see his daughter marry and ask if the young man is interested. Polygamy is legal for Muslims, although few urban Syrians practice it. Divorce is rare.

A Syrian bride in a Western-style wedding dress and traditional headscarf.

Bedouins and villagers are very traditional people. In many Syrian villages, a young woman's marital hopes are often expressed through the wedding dress she sews. The patterns of the dresses are set by village or clan tradition, although within those patterns each gown is slightly different. The traditional dress in most northern Syrian villages is heavy black material finely embroidered with scarlet patterns. The dress takes a year or longer to sew by hand and is often signed by the maker: her name is sewn into some part of the garment. The left side of the dress is often highly decorated, while the right side has only coarse, simple designs. This is because the baby is traditionally carried on the right arm. The woman usually wears the dress for several years.

Since marriage is the main goal in life, wedding parties are major social events. Among traditional people, the bride parties with her mother, sisters, female cousins, and friends in a house. They sing, dance, talk, laugh, and eat for hours. The bridegroom does the same with his male friends and relatives. The festivities may go on all night long in the city, all afternoon and evening in a village.

Wealthy people often rent a hotel ballroom or entire restaurant, and after some separate-gender celebration, the whole group may come together to eat, talk, and dance all night.

Depending on the custom of the area, the wedding party might take place either before the actual wedding or after it. Among the most traditional people, the families await confirmation from the groom, after the wedding night, that the new wife was a virgin. If she was not, or seems not to be, the marriage could be ended immediately and the woman severely punished by her family.

GENDER ROLES

The constitution adopted at the founding of the Baath Party in 1947 stated: "The Arab woman enjoys all the rights of citizenship." This position sets Syria apart from most other Arab countries. Syrian women today enjoy full legal rights, and the government has promoted equal opportunities for women. Nonetheless, traditional restraints have prevented most women from taking advantage of these opportunities.

For more than two thousand years, Arab culture considered women to be inferior and girls to be of less value than boys. Women are still viewed as weaker than men in mind, body, and spirit and therefore are in need of male protection. The highly valuable and easily damaged honor of men depends largely on that of their women, especially on that of their sisters, so they are carefully protected. The slightest implication of unavenged impropriety on the part of the women in a family or of male infractions of the code of honesty and hospitality could irreparably destroy the honor of a family.

Despite traditionally being considered inferior to men, Syrian women today enjoy higher legal status than women in most other countries of the Middle East. They also have more freedom and are more respected compared to a few generations ago. There are women cabinet members and quite a few women in the Peoples' Legislative Assembly. However, few women work and only a handful hold powerful government positions. In 2012, two women headed the Ministry of Tourism and the Ministry of State for Environmental Affairs.

MOURNING A LOSS

When someone is near death, a common phrase is "To Allah we belong and to Allah we return." After someone dies, there are three days of *hidad*, or mourning, during which friends, relatives, and neighbors visit the family. Close female relatives are expected to wear black for many months after the death. After a period of time, they can start wearing half black and half white. For very traditional families, it may be a year or longer before the women can wear colors again. For more modern families, the time is usually at least six months. If an older woman's husband dies and she is not likely to remarry, she may wear black for the rest of her life. These mourning traditions are similar in both Christian and Muslim families.

THE LEARNING ENVIRONMENT

Syria is striving to educate all its citizens, and literacy has increased dramatically in the last twenty years. Literacy today is high in Syria, with 91.7 percent of men and 81 percent of women able to read and write.

Leading up to 2011, the education system in Syria was highly praised. Public school is free, and students are required to complete up to ninth grade.

A new educational curriculum was introduced by the Syrian government in 2012, revitalizing many subjects. However, in some parts of the country, depending on which armed group is in power, certain subjects are not taught, such as national history. In the Homs area, the national flag and pictures of Assad are banned, while in Damascus, which is under regime control, pro-government propaganda is everywhere. In some major cities, many schools

A Syrian woman reads on a terrace overlooking Aleppo.

operate two shifts each day to accommodate an influx of students. In Aleppo, the first shift runs from 8 a.m. to 11:30 a.m., with the second shift starting at 12 p.m. and continuing until 3:30 p.m.

School enrollment has suffered greatly during the war. While before the conflict nearly all Syrian children attended classes, many schools have shut down. As of September 2015, two million Syrian children were not attending school. More than five thousand schools have been closed since 2011. Some have been destroyed in attacks, while others have been turned into shelters and military bases. Even in the face of violence, many young Syrians have forged on with their education; in 2015, at least 20 percent of students crossed areas of conflict to take their final exams. The Syrian Ministry of Education is working in partnership with UNICEF on the Back to Learning initiative, which provides students with school supplies and teaches Arabic, English, science, and math. The program strives to reach one million children within Syria.

Syria has four universities, and students pay only a token annual fee to attend. The largest is the University of Damascus, followed by the University

Kurdish students return to their studies at a school damaged by the conflict.

Many of the Syrians fleeing the war are university students. Once outside the country, it is difficult for them to continue their studies with little money and in nations with different languages and education systems.

In response to this need, Syrians in exile, led by former law professor Mosab al-Jamal, opened the Free Syrian University in Reyhanli, near the Syria-Turkey border, in 2013. Among its thirteen majors, students can study law, psychology, and business. Many Syrian professors living in both Turkey and abroad are teaching, or have offered to teach, courses. Over 870 students attend classes in a three-story apartment building, while others complete their schoolwork over the Internet.

Al-Jamal describes the universities in Syria as "prisons for students ... They capture or arrest anyone who opposes the regime." As an educator, al-Jamal see it as his responsibility to help Syrian students continue their education. For many students of the Syrian Free University, continuing with their studies carries hope for Syria when they are able to return: "If [the students who left their studies] come back to Syria ignorant and illiterate, they won't be able to help their country."

of Aleppo. There are also universities in Latakia and Homs. Many students also go abroad to study. There are also agricultural and technical schools for vocational training.

University students can study whatever they want with this exception: only the top percentage of high school students (based on special exams) are allowed to study medicine, and only the next best tier is allowed to study engineering. Neither group of students is required to study in those fields, but they usually do. This creates a situation where the brightest students are most often doctors, dentists, or engineers.

RESIDENCES

Most city dwellers live in apartments; many of them live in condominiums that are owned by the occupants. Syrian cities have no such thing as single-family homes, except for the mansions of ambassadors and top government

Courtyard houses are a distinct architectural style found in the old quarter of cities such as Damascus and Aleppo. While this style has modernized over time, it is rooted in the nomadic tradition of setting up tents around a central space. Today, with a modest exterior and extravagant interior, these residences have been nicknamed the "architecture of the veil."

The entryways to the courtyard houses are simple, yet once a person steps into the courtyard, he or she encounters an elaborately decorated space, teeming with colorful flowers and citrus trees. A fountain or well is often a central showpiece.

The entrance to the house is usually decorated with geometric patterns. The ground floor, called the haramlek, *is the main living space. Sleeping quarters are located on the second floor. One distinct feature is the* mushrabiya, *a balcony with a screened space for women, which allows them privacy, as is customary in many Muslim homes.*

officials. Many wealthy and upper-middle-class people build large vacation homes (called villas) in the mountains or near the sea. Some of these are relatively modest, but most are quite extravagant.

The focal point of rural houses is most often the front door. It may be huge compared to the house and is frequently decorated with geometric patterns and painted in multiple colors. In the western part of the country, nearly all rural houses are surrounded by olive trees and grapevines. Many houses have grape arbors over the roof to keep the hot summer sun off the house while at the same time creating favorable conditions to help ripen the grapes.

URBAN LIVING

Most of the population of Syria lives in cities. The cities have several distinct sections. The ancient core of a city usually represents the pre-Greek or pre-Roman period, with sections added in Greek, Roman, and medieval times. Newer sections were built during the French occupation.

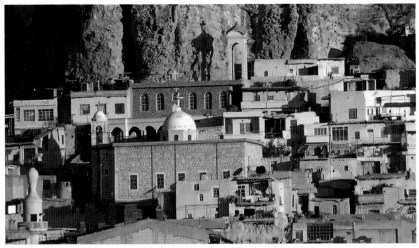

The village of Maaloula is built into the rocky side of a mountain.

Cities were traditionally organized into ethnic and religious residential quarters. Members of the different faiths still tend to live together, and the quarter functions as a small community within the larger urban setting. A residential quarter traditionally had its own mosque or other religious structure, shops, and coffeehouses. Many wealthier families live in the modern parts of the cities, where neighborhoods are divided along economic lines rather than by religious or ethnic affiliation.

Since 2011, many people have migrated to Syria's major cities. This influx has created a housing shortage. Many buildings that have been damaged in the conflict have been repurposed to house the growing number of Syrians seeking jobs and safety in the nation's cities.

RURAL LIFE

Although more and more people from villages are finishing high school and even attending college, basic village life in Syria has not changed much over the centuries. Villages have less wealth than the cities; there are relatively few cars, and the ancient Arab cultural attributes are more noticeable here than in the cities. Villagers' lifestyles are closer to those of the Bedouins than to those of city dwellers. The villagers are less accustomed to foreigners and are more conservative. These traits are especially noticeable in villages in the desert and along the Euphrates River.

The Bedouins have spent hundreds of years fashioning a life out of the harsh desert landscape.

Most Syrian villages have electricity, some indoor plumbing, schools, and clinics, but these amenities are not universal. Where there is no official school, the local mosque or church serves as one.

In villages and rural areas, most people live in small, one- to three-room homes with a small courtyard, the older ones generally made from adobe bricks and plaster. Each village has a few villas built by villagers who have made money in the city or by local farmers who have been successful.

NOMADS OF THE DESERT

As for indigenous peoples throughout the world, the traditional lifestyle of the Bedouins has changed a great deal. This is not the result of colonialism, as it has been with most other indigenous peoples, but rather the result of the encroachment of modern living.

The traditional Bedouins' entire existence revolves around raising sheep and herding them from one sparse feeding ground to another in millennia-old seasonal cycles.

There are now three types of Bedouins: settled, seminomadic, and fully nomadic. The settled Bedouins live at the edge of the steppe or desert, where there is enough water for them to grow crops. Seminomads spend winter in villages and the rest of the year grazing their sheep. The fully nomadic groups live in their black goatskin tents all year, moving whenever they must to provide grazing for their sheep.

Two factors are destroying the traditional nomadic lifestyle. The first is modern technology in the form of trucks and tankers that haul sheep to market and water to sheep, circumventing natural watering holes and "sheep drives" to market. The second factor is the control that the government of Syria has gained during the last half a century over the tribal feuding and warfare that were common among clans for thousands of years. Now, instead of fighting with one another and keeping sheep to a level that allowed quick mobility, the Bedouins try to raise much larger flocks of sheep. In a fragile environment, these practices have caused severe overgrazing and have diminished the ability of the land to support sheep.

In the spring, when grazing is good in the desert and steppe, Bedouin tents are everywhere, and parked beside most of them is not a camel but a large sheep-hauling truck and maybe even a generator. Many tents have televisions that run off the generator or truck. Children are often bussed to the village school.

Population growth and climate change have also contributed to the demise of traditional Bedouin life. Better health care has increased their life-span at the same time that the land supports less life. Young Bedouins often end up in villages or cities where they farm, do construction work, clean streets, or do any other work they can find.

INTERNET LINKS

carnegieendowment.org/syriaincrisis/?fa=60264
The Carnegie Endowment for International Peace takes an in-depth look at the history of the Bedouins in Syria and the role they play in the current conflict.

www.csmonitor.com/World/Middle-East/2009/1213/Behind-the-veil-Why-Islam-s-most-visible-symbol-is-spreading
The *Christian Science Monitor* examines the role of the headscarf in Islamic culture.

www.muslimheritage.com/article/courtyard-houses-syria
Take a look inside some of Syria's unique courtyard houses.

nadiamuhanna.wordpress.com/2009/11/01/the-big-day
On this page, people share their stories of Syrian wedding customs.

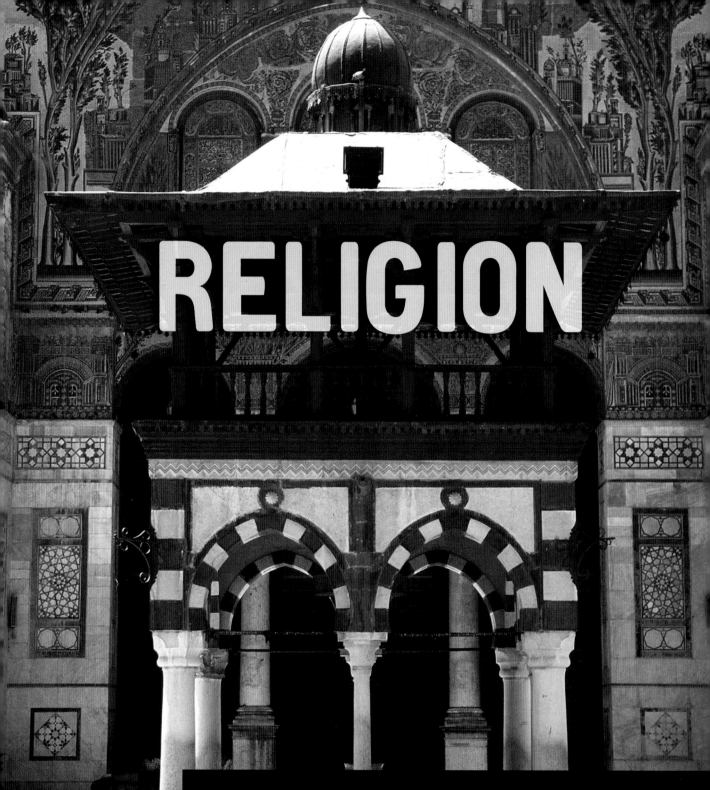

RELIGION

The Omayyad Mosque is one of the world's oldest and holiest sites.

8

THE RELIGIOUS MAKEUP OF SYRIA IS A mosaic of beliefs. Religious tolerance has been a cornerstone of Syrian culture for decades. However, as conflict in the country and around the world has escalated, what was once celebrated as a tolerant and secular society has seen divisions deepen along religious lines.

Although Syria has a large assortment of religious groups, including Muslims, Christians, and Jews, these groups all share a strong belief in God. Syrians' greetings, good-byes, and many other common expressions give credit to God for everything, thank God for everything, and leave the future up to God. The most common response when you ask someone how he or she is is *al Hamdulla* (al-HAM-dool-la), which means "Thank Allah!" When Syrians learn English, they translate these expressions into "God bless you," "God willing," and "Thank God."

Religion is part of everyday life in Syria, and most people wear their beliefs proudly. There are hundreds of churches in Syria, and all religions are guaranteed freedom of worship by the country's constitution. Syrian laws do not allow proselytizing—trying to convert others to your own religious beliefs.

Muslims constitute about 87 percent of the population. Of this, 74 percent are members of the Sunni sect, and Alawites, Ismaili, and Shia account for the rest. Other Shia groups constitute less than 1 percent of the population. Druzes, members of an offshoot of Islam, account for 3 percent of the population, and Christians for 10 percent. There are also

Often referred to as "devil worshipers," the Kurdish-speaking Yazidis are a commonly misunderstood religious sect. Making their homes in the mountains of northwest Iraq, northwest Syria, and southeast Turkey, there are an estimated seventy thousand to five hundred thousand followers of this ancient religion.

Yazidis worship a supreme being called Yasdan. They also recognize seven angels, led by Melek Taus, also called the Peacock Angel. Yazidis pray to this divine angel five times each day. Their belief system holds that they descended from Adam, not Eve, and religious doctrine forbids certain foods, such as pork, and dressing in blue. Wednesdays are the holy day for Yazidis, and both the Bible and Qur'an are considered sacred texts.

The Yazidis form a tightly knit, closed community. Followers must be born into the faith, and they marry within the sect. They do not believe in the concept of hell, instead believing in reincarnation. Each September, a pilgrimage is made to the shrine of Sheikh Adi ibn Musafir, the religion's founder, in Lalesh, north of Mosul, Iraq.

small groups of Jews and Yazidis, a sect that combines elements of Judaism, Christianity, and Islam, as well as older religious beliefs.

EARLY BELIEFS

Before the Muslim Omayyads conquered Syria in the eighth century, there had been many religions in the land. The Phoenicians, Assyrians, Babylonians, Greeks, and Romans all spread their own particular beliefs in different parts of Syria. The ancient beliefs were eventually replaced by the monotheism (belief in one God) of Judaism, Christianity, and Islam.

A GOD OF MANY PEOPLES

The name Ba'al (BAY-el) was first used in approximately the same sense Christians now use the word "Lord." Many gods were referred to as Ba'al among the Semitic people of the Middle East: the Sumerian god of the air, Enlil; Marduk, God of Babylon; Asshur, god of Assyria; and others. An Arabic expression for a polytheist—one who believes in more than one god—is ashra baalla (AHSH-ra BAAL-la), literally "ten gods." The Phoenicians initially used Ba'al as a title for their god of storms, Hadad, but it later became his name. Ba'al is an old word in both Hebrew and Arabic that means "husband," "master," and "owner." Ba'al Zebub, the healing god of Ekron, later became one word—Beelzebub—which came to represent evil and idolatry in the New Testament of the Bible.

One Canaanite myth claimed that Ba'al reigned during the growing season of the year and died thereafter. His place was taken by Mot, the god of death and sterility, who represented the hot, dry summers. Anat, Ba'al's wife and sister, searched for him during the reign of Mot, found him, and brought him back from death. That is how the autumn rains began.

Although the Hebrews purportedly believed only in Yahweh, they often adopted other "Ba'als" from the Canaanites. Jezebel, the Phoenician wife of King Ahab of the Hebrews, is an example of a Ba'al worshipper.

THE BIRTH OF ISLAM

Although Judaism and Christianity are native to Greater Syria and have been there for thousands of years, Islam filled the land not only with its beliefs but also with the language of its holy book—the Qur'an—within a hundred years of its inception.

In 570 CE, the Prophet Muhammad was born to a noble Arab family in Mecca, an area that was then called the Hejaz. He spent most of his life as a merchant, but it is said that when he was forty years old and in solitary meditation, he was visited by the angel Gabriel. The angel began giving him God's words—in Arabic—which eventually became the Qur'an. Muhammad began spreading this new "revelation," attracting both followers and enemies among the people of Mecca. Hostility and persecution from the Meccans eventually forced him and his followers to flee to Medina in 622. This migration marks the beginning of the Muslim year. For eight years, Muhammad headed Islam from Medina, returning to Mecca in 630. Although he died two years later and was buried in Medina, Mecca became the most holy city for Muslims, and the Kaaba Mosque its most holy place.

Early Islam was intensely expansionist. Conquering armies and migrating tribes spread out of Arabia. Syria was among the first countries to come under its sway. By 635, Muslim armies had conquered Damascus.

DIVISIONS OF ISLAM

Today, the vast majority of Syrians are Muslim. Most of these are Sunni Muslims, while the rest are Shias, Druzes, Alawites, and Ismailis. "Islam" means "submission to Allah." Muslims consider their religion to be a continuation of Judaism and Christianity, with Muhammad as the last of the prophets and the Qur'an (also called "The Book") superseding all other revelations from God. In the Qur'an, Muslims, Jews, and Christians are all referred to as "children of the Book."

Muslims believe that Jesus Christ was a prophet and that his teachings are not superseded by the Qur'an. They think it is blasphemous to believe that God, an all-encompassing spirit, could have a human son. Instead, they believe that Christ's claim to being the son of God is figurative.

Unlike Christianity, where virtually all sects and varieties have an official leader, the followers of Islam do not have a hierarchy of authority. Each mosque has its holy man—called a sheikh—who holds his position as spiritual guide by virtue of his study of Islam and his perceived piety.

RELIGIOUS BREAKDOWN

Syria's largest religious minority are the Alawites, who account for about 12 percent of the population. They live mainly along the coast in Latakia Province, where they constitute much of the rural population. The Alawites are descendants of people who have lived in this region since the time of Alexander the Great. They were gradually influenced by Islam and Christianity. Although they claim to be Muslims, conservative Sunnis do not always recognize

THE FIVE PILLARS OF ISLAM

The Qur'an and the teachings and life of the Prophet guide every aspect of Muslim life. Everything from government to commerce to life's daily rituals and details are covered. The most prominent religious principles, called the Five Pillars of Islam, are as follows:

1. Shahada *(sha-HAA-da)*: The declaration that there is only one God and that Muhammad was his last prophet.

2. Salat *(sa-LAAT)*: Prayer five times daily—at sunrise, midday, afternoon, sunset, and evening. The supplicant must face Mecca, and women must cover their hair and entire bodies (except the face, in some sects).

    Throughout the Muslim world, chanted calls to prayer are broadcast from all mosques and become part of the rhythm of life. Before electricity, a muezzin would mount the steps of the minarets (mosque towers) and issue the call. Now the calls to prayer are recordings broadcast over loudspeakers. The chanting is still hauntingly beautiful.

3. Zakat *(za-KAT)*: An annual tithe of 2.5 percent of earnings above basic necessities. This is used to build and maintain mosques and help the poor.

4. Sawm *(soom)*: Fasting during Ramadan—the ninth month of the Islamic year.

5. Hajj *(haaj)*: The pilgrimage to Mecca, with a stop in Medina to pay respects at the Prophet's grave. This is required once in a lifetime, but only if the person has the financial means to do so.

The interiors of many mosques are decorated with intricate artwork and high ceilings.

them as such. Like Christians, the Alawites celebrate Christmas, Easter, and Epiphany and use sacramental wine in some ceremonies.

Because many of the tenets of the faith are secret, Alawites have refused to discuss their faith with outsiders. Only a few of their number learn the religion after a lengthy initiation. Only the men take part in worship.

The Alawites formerly were the poorest of the religious groups. As Hafez al-Assad rose to power in 1971, they became the largest group in the military, holding most of the officer positions. Under the Baath regime, the Alawites have been favored, causing much resentment among Syria's Sunni majority and among its other minority groups.

The Druze community constitutes 3 percent of the population and forms the majority in the Jabal al-Arab region (formerly Jabal al-Druze), a mountainous area in southwestern Syria. The Druze religion is a tenth-century offshoot of Islam, but Muslims view the Druzes as heretical. The Druzes have always kept their doctrine and rituals secret to avoid persecution. Only those who demonstrate great piety and devotion are initiated into its mysteries. The initiated are a very small minority but may include women. Although women are veiled in public, they are permitted to participate in the councils of elders.

The Ismailis are an offshoot of Shia Islam, the result of a disagreement over the seventh imam. There are around two hundred thousand Ismailis in Syria. Originally settled in Latakia Province, they now live mostly south of Salamiyah on land granted to their community by a sultan of the Ottoman Empire.

CHRISTIANITY

The major Christian sects in the country are Syrian Orthodox, Greek Orthodox, and Armenian Orthodox. There are also quite a few Roman Catholics and a

SUNNI AND SHIA

The bulk of Syrians belong to the Sunni sect, with a small number of Shia Muslims. These two sects are the result of a schism in Islam that occurred in the seventh century. After the death of Ali, the Prophet's son-in-law and fourth successor, or caliph, there was a disagreement over who should succeed him. Muawiyah, the governor of Syria, proclaimed himself caliph, beginning the line of Omayyad caliphs, who ruled from Damascus. The Shiat Ali, or followers of Ali, refused to recognize his legitimacy and established a dissident sect that became known as the Shia. They believe that the caliph must be descended from the Prophet. The major faction of Islam, the Sunni, believe that the caliph should be elected. This amounts to a division between partisans of leadership by consensus and partisans of divine right.

This tenth-century manuscript shows Caliph Muawiyah I.

Today, the Sunni sect includes the majority of Muslims around the world. The Shia sect is centered in Iran and Iraq, where Ali moved his capital. Syria, the homeland of the Omayyad caliphs, is overwhelmingly Sunni.

handful of Protestants and Russian Orthodox Christians. The Syrian Orthodox Church still celebrates Mass in Aramaic, the ancient language of Christ. Christians account for about 10 percent of the religious population. Christmas and both Easters—Western and Orthodox—are official government holidays.

Most Syrian Christians live in or near the coastal mountains. A drive through the mountains reveals many villages with a church or two but no mosques. These mountains also contain numerous monasteries and convents, some very old as well as some new. Christians are usually city dwellers; many live near Damascus, Aleppo, Hama, and Latakia. They tend to be well educated and relatively affluent, working more often in the professions.

The best-known Christian to live in Syria was Saint Paul, one of the main authors of the New Testament. It was on the road from Palestine to Damascus that he was converted from Judaism to Christianity, and he lived in Damascus for nearly two decades. He preached in the Jewish synagogues of Syria for several years. When some Jews plotted to kill him, he escaped by being  *lowered from a house built on the wall of the ancient city of Damascus. Part of this wall is still standing. Also, a main street in the old city is still called by the same name as in Paul's time—The Street Called Straight (above)—and it is the only straight street that travels all the way through the old city.*

With the exception of the Armenians and Assyrians, most Christians are Arabs, sharing the same Arabic traditions with their Muslim counterparts.

SECRET RELIGIOUS SITES

At the beginning of Christianity, most of what is now Syria was part of the Roman Empire. The Romans were tolerant of the religions of the people they conquered, as long as those people did not threaten the empire and at least gave occasional sacrifices to Roman gods. Much later, Christian belief was outlawed and made a capital offense.

Christians were secretive and aloof, would not serve the empire in any way, and engaged in practices that made nonbelievers suspicious. This led to increasing persecution during the second and third centuries CE. Thousands of Christian believers escaped to the eastern side of the coastal mountains and lived in caves to hide from their persecutors. Just outside Damascus, there are many cave houses carved into hillsides, sometimes high up where they can only be reached by ladder.

The largest concentration of caves is in Maaloula, north of Damascus and close to the modern border of Lebanon. Hundreds of cave houses were carved into the limestone cliffs here, and its inhabitants even buried their dead in a cave cemetery.

Some superstitious Syrians believe in the "evil eye" and carry small charms such as a miniature Qur'an or blue eye to ward off this unfriendly gaze.

INTERNET LINKS

www.cfr.org/peace-conflict-and-human-rights/sunni-shia-divide/ p33176#!/?cid=otr-marketing_url-sunni_shia_infoguide
The Council on Foreign Relations provides a comprehensive history of the Shia-Sunni divide.

religion.blogs.cnn.com/2013/09/04/syrian-wars-got-religion-and-that-aint-good
The CNN religion blog explains how Syria's war has become divided along religious lines.

www.sacred-destinations.com/syria/sacred-sites
This website provides information on many of Syria's holy sites.

LANGUAGE

يا ابا الصالح المهدي (ع)

عجل على ظهورك

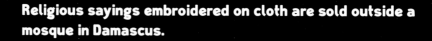

Religious sayings embroidered on cloth are sold outside a mosque in Damascus.

9

I N SYRIA, ARABIC IS THE PRINCIPAL language spoken by over 90 percent of the population. Among the country's other commonly spoken languages are Kurdish, Armenian, Aramaic, and Circassian. Many educated people also understand French or English.

Arabic is a Semitic language, along with Hebrew, Aramaic, Syriac, and other ancient tongues of the Middle East. Arabs have a rich oral tradition, and according to some Arab scholars, the oral mastery of even illiterate desert and village Arabs is extraordinary. The use of language is the supreme Arab art form.

The differences between Arabic and English are so great that native speakers of one who become fluent in the other often continue to have

Arabic is the language used in the Qur'an, the holy book of Islam, pictured here.

trouble with the very different rhetorical styles. These differing styles form the cultural gulf and the different views of life that divide Arabic- and English-speaking peoples.

AN ANCIENT LANGUAGE

Arabic is an ancient language. Its roots date back thousands of years, and because of its holy status in the Qur'an, it has likely evolved less over the last thousand years than any other major language. Arab traders spread Arabic into Africa and India hundreds of years ago, and languages of both those areas bear some similarities to Arabic. Somali and Swahili in particular contain a lot of Arabic-based words.

A number of English words originated in Arabic. Some examples are "alcohol," "algebra," "check," "checkmate," "lute," "magazine," "mosaic," "safari," "Sahara," "sheriff," "shish kabob," and "tariff." The numerals used in Europe and North America were also originally Arabic. Syrians, however, now use numerals brought to the country from India.

MORE THAN JUST WORDS

Native English speakers have developed the linguistic and cultural values of understatement, precision, use of logic, and brevity. In other words, say what you mean clearly, and no more. Native Arabic speakers, on the other hand, have developed the cultural and linguistic values of emotional appeal, overstatement or exaggeration, repetition, and words in lieu of action.

APPEALING TO EMOTIONS Some Arabists, scholars who study Arab culture, have claimed that Arabs are swayed more by words than by ideas, more by ideas than by facts. Educated native English speakers might be impressed and their thinking influenced by a logical argument loaded with facts and figures; an Arab—either educated or illiterate—will most often be impressed and won over by powerful emotional arguments.

This difference can create a communication barrier. Some Arabs may feel that the cool, detached, fact-filled arguments of a Westerner lack emotional appeal. In a way, this reflects the use of English as a "business and technical" language. However, there are exceptions to the way Arabic is used. For example, newspapers and scientific journals would use more "precise" Arabic, whereas traditional poetry and literature use a more flowery form of the language.

OVERSTATING AND REPEATING   Writing style also varies greatly between English and Arabic. Compared to typical precise English, Arabic is flowery, wordy, and repetitive. Arabic writing often says the same thing over and over in slightly different ways.

Overstatement is also used for politeness. If you say *marhaba* (MAR-ha-ba) or *ahlan* (ah-LAWN), meaning "hello," to a Syrian, the answer will usually be *marhabtain* (mar-hab-TAIN) or *ahlain* (ah-LAIN), meaning "two hellos," or *ahlan wa sahlan* (ah-LAWN-wa-sah-LAWN), meaning "hello and welcome." In other words, the response outdoes the initial greeting.

Syrians use body language to reinforce what they are saying. This man is bartering with a vendor at a market in Aleppo.

Here are some common words and phrases for those new to Arabic.

Hello	ahlan
Welcome	ahlan wa sahlan
Goodbye	ila al'likaa'
Thank you	shukran
You're welcome	a'afwan
How are you?	kaifa haluka?
My name is …	ana ismee …
Do you speak English?	hal tatakallam al ingliziya?

WORDS NOT ACTION Another characteristic of Arabic foreign to most native English speakers is the use of threats without action. If Syrians make a threat, they are unlikely to carry out the action. However, people from a culture where idle threats are not often made perceive the threat as real and act accordingly.

Conversely, when Arab enemies (perceived or real) say nothing, that is the time to worry. In Arab villages and among nomadic tribes, "honor" and vengeance killings, though now illegal, often take place with no warning at all when a family feels it has been dishonored.

MANY DIALECTS

Spoken Arabic dialects are more diverse than English dialects worldwide—so much so, in fact, that a Damascene has trouble understanding an Egyptian, and an Omani and a Moroccan can understand very little of each other's speech.

The differences in dialects are not only in pronunciation and intonation but in the use of different words. A Syrian shopping for vegetables in Morocco would find that familiar produce has a different name; the Moroccan would

SAVING ARAMAIC

Aramaic is the world's oldest living language, and it heralds from the time of Jesus Christ. Christ's famous final words during his crucifixion, "Eli, Eli, lama sabachtani" ("My God, my God, why hast thou forsaken me") were spoken in Aramaic. UNESCO has classified Aramaic as an endangered language. It uses letters similar to those found in Hebrew.

Over thirty years ago, in Syria, it was forbidden to speak Aramaic. In 2008, the Aramaic Language Academy was founded by the University of Damascus in Maaloula, a small town located about 35 miles (56 km) northeast of the capital. About seven thousand people speak Aramaic in Maaloula, plus another eight thousand in two nearby villages. The Assad government provided funding for the new school, which offered classes to eighty-five students studying at three different levels.

Only a few short years later, in September 2013, the war reached Maaloula. Many fled the village as it fell under control of an extremist Islamic group. In spring 2014, the Syrian government regained control of what remained of Maaloula. Many homes, churches, and monasteries all lay in ruin.

There is a fear that Aramaic will die out as its few speakers have scattered around the globe. Efforts are being made to preserve the language for future generations. In 2013, a British linguist began work to record the language, before it disappears forever. A German professor has compiled an Aramaic dictionary and also established a charitable organization to raise funds to rebuild Maaloula when it is safe for its residents to return home.

not understand the Syrian words for the vegetables. The Egyptian dialect is well known for using a lot of words that are different from other dialects.

Even from city to city, there are noticeable variations, and the farther apart the cities are, the greater the difference. The dialect in Deir ez-Zor (on the Euphrates River) is quite different from that in Damascus, a little more than 300 miles (483 km) away.

ARABIC IN WRITING

The Arabic used today for most kinds of writing and certain types of formal speaking is classical Arabic, which is the language of the Qur'an. Classical Arabic is the same for all speakers of Arabic regardless of region. With the increase in literacy in the Arab world, classical Arabic is becoming more widely used, and some Arab thinkers and leaders hope that eventually it will replace local dialects.

Arabic is written and read from right to left. There are no capital letters, but many letters change form depending on their position in a word. In addition, there are several different styles of writing that use different shapes for some letters.

The ancient style of written Arabic is quite elaborate and decorative and difficult to read, even for most Arabs. The style used in newspapers and magazines, called modern standard Arabic, is easier to read except for someone learning the language. The reason is that the marks indicating short vowels (there are both short and long vowels) and double consonants (there are both single and double consonants) are not used in modern writing. Without these symbols, it is often difficult to know what word a person is reading. Imagine, for example, reading English with all short vowels omitted: "pen," "pin," "pan," and "pun" would all be spelled "pn!"

TONGUE TWISTERS

There are several Arabic sounds that have no equivalent in the English alphabet. They are as follows, showing the English letter or letters usually used in transliteration (writing a language with the alphabet of a different one):

H (*ha*): A heavy *h* sound.

kh (*kha*): Similar to the *ch* sound in the German *Bach*; the back of the tongue against the rear roof of the mouth does not completely block off the air flow.

S (*sahd*): A loose-tongued *s*; the tip of the tongue is not against the ridge behind the upper front teeth, but the front part of the tongue is flat against the front of the palate; somewhere between *sh* and *s* in English.

D (*dahd*): A loose-tongued *d*, same instructions as for *sahd*.

T (*taa*): A loose-tongued *t*; same as above.

Z (*zaa*): A loose-tongued *z*; same as above.

9 (*ayn*): A vowel formed with a narrowing of the throat; a lot of difference in intensity of this sound between some dialects.

gh (*ghayn*): Like a *g* without the back of the tongue actually touching the roof of the mouth; sometimes sounds like *l* or *r*.

' (*hamza*): A glottal (voice box) stop; like how someone in the Cockney dialect would say bottle (*bo'le*); the way most western Americans say *t* when immediately followed by *n*: important, *impor'ant*; button, *bu'n*.

q (*qaa*): A stop like a *k*, but made in the throat; Syrian dialect substitutes hamze for this.

HAND GESTURES AND BODY POSITION

When Syrians talk to each other, they stand close together and use lots of hand gestures. They tend to speak loudly as well. Such things are likely to make a newcomer think a fight is about to start, but this is not the case. Even what in the West would be considered an aggressive stance—standing close to and leaning toward another person—is normal in Syria.

Syrians also use head movements to communicate. A quick upward movement of the head with raised eyebrows, often accompanied by closed eyes and a click of the tongue, means "no." A downward nod to one side means "yes." Shaking the head from side to side (like a North American saying "no"), often accompanied by a puzzled look, means, "I don't understand," or "I didn't hear you."

THE KURDISH LANGUAGE

For decades, the Kurdish language and all languages other than Arabic have been banned from Syrian newspapers and schools. With the outbreak of the war, the Baath government began to loosen its hold on Kurdish regions. The Kurds took this as an opportunity to make small yet significant steps toward cultural independence.

In 2013, in the city of Qamishli, the first Kurdish newspaper was started.

Kurdish students study in a makeshift school in a Turkish refugee camp.

Appropriately named Nu Dem, *which translates from Kurdish to "New Time," the publication is entirely volunteer-driven and reaches a circulation of about three thousand. The paper is issued in Kurmanji, the most widespread dialect of the Kurdish people.*

For fifty-three years, it has been illegal to teach Kurdish in Syrian schools. Anyone caught doing so could be placed under arrest. Today, in areas that remain under Kurdish control, a new curriculum is being followed, which teaches Kurdish in first through third grade, as well as in upper years. For many, preserving their native language for the next generation provides an important link to Kurdish identity.

Hand gestures here are similar to those in Greece and Italy. Holding the palm turned up with fingertips together forming a tent over the palm while pumping the hand and forearm means, "Wait a minute." Holding the arms out to the side and raised as if to catch raindrops with the palms up and open means, "What's going on here?" Drawing the open hands up quickly above the shoulders, palms facing the other person, means, "That's my point," or

"That's my excuse." Brushing the open palms together quickly as if to brush off dirt signifies, "I'm finished with it (or with you)."

Another common gesture is patting the right hand over the heart when meeting someone. This shows affection for the person.

MANY TONGUES

English, French, German, and Russian are also spoken in Syria. Most educated people speak at least a little of one of these—students in high school can study English, French, and German. Most Syrians who speak another language live in Damascus. Rural areas and villages, particularly in eastern Syria, have few people who speak anything but their own Arabic dialect.

Some ancient languages are still spoken in Syria, although some—such as Aramaic—are under threat. In the far northwestern corner of the country, the Armenian language is so common that signs are in both Arabic and Armenian. There are a few speakers of Syriac (one of the original languages of Syria) and Kurdish in the northeastern part of the country. Some people in the north speak Turkish, and many Jews can speak or at least read Hebrew.

INTERNET LINKS

www.bbc.co.uk/languages/other/arabic/guide/phrases.shtml
The BBC Arabic guide for beginners includes an overview of the alphabet and common words supported by audio clips.

www.ethnologue.com/country/SY/languages
This website provides in-depth coverage of the languages spoken in Syria from its past to the present day. This site also includes a map showing where each language group is spoken.

www.youtube.com/watch?v=Iy38UQ9EQ6o
Watch a short video on Aramaic, filmed in Maaloula, and listen to many of the villagers speak this ancient language.

ARTS

The gates of an Omayyad castle welcome visitors to the National Museum in Damascus.

10

SYRIA HAS A RICH TRADITION OF arts, many using techniques that date back centuries. In modern times, art has become a creative medium through which many Syrians offer messages of hope and resistance in the shadow of ongoing unrest.

Galleries displaying Syrian artwork are housed at the National Museum in Damascus, which was founded in 1919.

ANCIENT ARTWORK

Syria's museums contain sculptures and ceramic art spanning many thousands of years. Most of the ancient art was related to function—things such as storage jars, bowls, vases, fighting shields, and images of fertility goddesses. The majority of art in these museums is Roman sculpture and remnants of mosaic floors. The Roman art of the Byzantine era (eastern Roman empire) differs noticeably from that of the western Roman empire (Europe).

With the widespread destruction and targeting of ancient artifacts by ISIL, many of these cultural treasures are being transported to more stable areas, such as Damascus. At the Aleppo National Museum, many statues have been surrounded by sandbags and encased in concrete to prevent against damage from explosive devices such as rockets and mortars. Several of the museum's curators are now living in the museum to offer what little protection they can to safeguard these artifacts of Syrian culture.

Syrian folktales are traditionally passed down orally from one generation to the next. Many of these stories are now being collected and written down. "The Story of Luck and Fate," adapted here from the book Folktales of Syria, *is one of these tales:*

There was once a man who was always trying to uncover what his future held. One night, a message in a dream instructed him to go to the laurel wood, where he would at last meet his Luck and Fate.

Along the road to the wood, a beautiful woman called to the man, proposing to him that they marry and share her immense wealth. The man carried on, and next encountered an old man near the opening to a mine. The old man spoke, saying he wanted the younger man to be the heir to his great wealth.

Next, the man saw a priest, who offered him the chance to become a great priest and a place in the Kingdom of God. For the third time, the man refused, and carried on to the laurel wood. Soon, the man saw a large group of people standing outside the gate of a mighty city. They stopped him and asked that he be their king. Again, the man refused, for his Luck and Fate waited in the laurel wood.

At last, the man reached the wood. Suddenly, a snarling black panther came running toward him. The man ran away in fear. The panther asked the man why he was running, and the man replied, "Because I am afraid you will eat me."

"But I am your Luck and Fate," replied the panther. The man now did not want to meet either his Luck or Fate, and told the panther he would return along the road to one of the wonderful futures he had been offered. The panther said, "What you have missed is gone. There is no escape from your Luck and Fate." The black cat then pounced on the man, eating him.

SYRIAN TEXTS

Syria has inherited a rich tradition of Arabic literature, in which poetry is a particularly important form. Public recital of odes was a common feature of Bedouin life, and the public reading of poetry continues to be part of Arab life.

Adunis has had an especially wide influence. He was born Ali Ahmad Said in 1930. He was influenced in his early days by the ideal of Syrian nationalism.

TO MECCA

When Muslims pray, they face and bow toward the birthplace of the Prophet—Mecca, which is in northwestern Saudi Arabia. The supplicants always pray on a carpet. The floors of all mosques are covered with carpets, and people who are praying elsewhere use a special prayer carpet. Some of these small rugs are made completely by hand by Bedouins. Many have arrowhead designs woven into them. When the carpet is laid down for prayer, the arrows point toward Mecca.

At about this time, he took his pen name, Adunis, which was the name of the mythical god of Syria who died in winter and was resurrected in the spring. As a student at Damascus University, he questioned both literary conventions and the social and political structure of Syria. He was imprisoned and then exiled to Beirut in 1956, where he has remained since.

Adunis maintains that only radical change in all aspects of life will bring the Arabs into the modern era. He uses poetry as a means of inducing revolutionary change to create a new society. In his search for revolutionary poetry, Adunis has developed a language that is allusive, evocative, and mystical—and often difficult to understand. Now in his eighties, while Adunis has been critical of the Assad regime, he has also made controversial remarks on the Syrian revolution as a whole. When asked during an interview in 2015 if he saw a solution for the crisis in Syria, the poet replied, "Syria is moving towards greater devastation. The revolution began in a good way—there was hope—but quickly it turned into a fight for power."

One of the most popular of contemporary Arab women writers is Ghada al-Samman, who was born in a Syrian village in 1942. She studied English literature in Damascus and London and then moved to Beirut. She went on to work as a journalist, poet, and novelist. Samman shares the preoccupations of many male writers—identity and loss of self, hatred of the harsh and unsettling social and economic conditions of the time, and the tension between tradition and modernity—but she also writes of the alienation she feels because of her femininity and her intellect.

THE SOUNDS OF SYRIA

A musician plays traditional Syrian music on the oud in a Lebanese restaurant that serves cuisine from Aleppo.

Arab people respond in a similar manner to both language and music, and there are many similarities between the two. The language is repetitive and exaggerated, and so is the music; the language is rich in subtleties, and so is the music; and the language is rich in storytelling tradition about honor, family, and love, and so is the music.

Arabic music is unlike any other and is dramatically different from Western music. It has varying sounds and incorporates many different instruments. There are two types of native music in Syria. Classical music uses the oud, the flute, and small, lap-held drums, sometimes without a lot of vocal accompaniment. Modern music uses an orchestra of mostly European instruments with one lead vocalist and a backup chorus.

Arabic music has had a heavy influence on other music around the Mediterranean, Africa, and in southern Asia—areas that were part of the Arab empire during the eighth to the tenth centuries. Indian music, for example, has a similar texture, and Spanish flamenco music is a direct descendant of classical Arabic music.

BREATHTAKING BUILDINGS

Islamic art finds its greatest expression in its mosques. The Omayyad Mosque is one of the most important buildings in the Muslim world. It was built on sacred ground that was first the site of a temple for Hadad, the Aramaean god of the ancient Syrians three thousand years ago, and of a pagan temple of Jupiter the Damascene during the Roman era. The temple later became a Byzantine church dedicated to Saint John the Baptist.

In 705 CE, when Damascus was the capital of the Arab Islamic empire, Omayyad Caliph al-Walid Abdul Malek cleared the site to erect an impressive mosque suited to the grandeur of the Arab state. The mosque has walls lined with marble overlaid with golden vines and a wooden roof inlaid with gold, while from the ceiling hang six hundred gold lamps. It is the finest example of Omayyad art, which spread from Damascus throughout the Islamic empire and became a major influence on the Muslim world.

The Citadel of Aleppo is probably the greatest military edifice of the Middle Ages. Much of the present building was built in the twelfth century by the Ayyubids. The souks of Aleppo, which cover 15 miles (24 km), date from the sixteenth and seventh centuries and are considered to be some of the most beautiful in the world. These picturesque old souks are specialized markets, such as the jewelry souk, spice souk, and carpet souk.

The Azem Palace was built in 1749 as the residence of one of the Ottoman governors of Damascus, Assaad Pacha el-Azem. It is considered to be one of the finest examples of eighteenth-century Arab architecture. Each room is designed to typical Damascene traditions, including separate quarters for the *haremlek*, the *selamlek*, and the *liwan*.

Since Islam forbids representational art in its mosques, Syrian decoration has concentrated on intricate geometric and floral patterns. The mosaic tile work of the mosques is particularly impressive. Calligraphy, or decorative writing, is also used frequently in Islamic art.

Vendors sell spices and other goods at the souk in Aleppo in 2012. Much of the market now lies in ruin.

CRAFTED BY HAND

Many Syrian handicrafts showcase designs and details that are unique to the country.

JEWELRY Syrian gold and silver work is extravagant. Bedouins have a centuries-old tradition of making elaborate jewelry for women, and this tradition is evident in modern jewelry. Middle- and upper-class Syrian women wear lots of jewelry: huge, sparkling earrings that often look like small chandeliers, large rings, and lots of bracelets, some meticulously filigreed.

These are made from gold, brass, or a gold-tone metal; the educated city-dwellers are very class conscious and do not wear silver. It is the Bedouin and village women who wear silver, and most antique Bedouin jewelry is made of silver. Bedouin women and some village women also wear jewelry in or on their head covers and veils, in the form of delicate chains and coin-like decorations. Elaborate utensils, trays, and baskets are also made by jewelers.

OTHER METAL WORK Brass and copper plates, bowls, and pitchers are common and lovely. The copper work is disappearing, though; it is a tradition of the rapidly dwindling Syrian Jewish population. There are also water pipes and large coffee servers (samovars) made from filigreed brass and copper.

Gold and silver coins sewn on a veil show a Bedouin woman's wealth.

WOODWORK Another Syrian specialty is inlaid woodwork. There are two basic types: one uses thin layers of factory-made veneers; the other has the wood, bone, or mother-of-pearl cut and set by hand. The craftspeople who do the latter can be seen at work in their shops, painstakingly cutting and fitting the tiny pieces.

There is wide variation in the quality and design of woodwork. Some inlays have only different-colored woods, while others contain bone or mother-of-pearl (most of it now artificial). There are boxes of every shape and size, trays, tables, game boards ranging from lap size to large tabletop models, and even desks made from marquetry.

FABRICS

The fabric arts of Syria take the form of clothing, tablecloths, pillowcases, and carpets. Most carpets made here are created by the Bedouins on horizontal, hand-built looms. The large ones are used to cover the floors of their tents, and small ones are used as prayer rugs. Particularly beautiful rugs are hung on the walls.

POWERFUL PICTURES: ALI FERZAT

Perhaps the best-known present-day Syrian artist, Ali Ferzat was born in the central city of Hama in 1951. The political cartoonist worked for state-owned newspapers and was always careful to not overstep in his criticism of Syrian politics. His bold style and comic portrayals earned him recognition within Syria and from the international community.

In 2011, as tensions began to rise in Syria and violence against civilians increased, the artist's work began to change. Ferzat began to draw cartoons that openly criticized the Baath government, including President Assad. Just a few months later, Ferzat was attacked in the streets of Damascus by a group loyal to the president. He was badly beaten and the bones in both of his hands were shattered.

Ferzat now lives in Kuwait. For his bravery in publicly opposing the oppressive Syrian government, Ferzat was award the Sakharov Prize for Freedom of Thought in 2011. A year later, Time *named the cartoonist as one of the top one hundred most influential people of 2012.*

Traditional garments with a great variety of embroidery, such as dresses, capes, jackets, and various sorts of gowns for both men and women, are still made by Bedouins and villagers. Syrian clothes tend to be brightly colored with an amazing profusion of designs—especially men's shirts and women's clothing. Here, Syrian creativity seems completely uninhibited.

Tablecloths and pillowcases with unique Damascene designs are now embroidered by machine but are still intricate and striking in appearance.

There is a special fabric known as damask, named for Damascus. Damascus was on the ancient Silk Route between China and India and the

During the Middle Ages, sword makers in Damascus became famous all over the Middle East, central Asia, and southern Europe for their swords. Through a lengthy and arduous process, these weapons were made so sharp they could cut a floating spider web, so hard they could cut through the shaft of a spear, yet so flexible they could be bent 90 degrees and spring back into shape. The secret alloy from which the swords were made was called Damascene steel.

But these were more than weapons: they were works of art. Through a process called Damascening, the handles were incised with elaborate patterns. The cuts were then inlaid with bronze, gold, and silver.

In the fourteenth century, one of Damascus's many conquerors carried off all the sword makers and put them in his own service, and the art of Damascene steel soon died out. The process of inlaying, however, lives on even today in the elaborate and intricate workmanship of both metal and woodcrafts.

West. The original damask, developed hundreds of years ago, was made exclusively from silk interwoven with silver and gold threads. In the eleventh century, crusaders brought it back to Europe, where it became popular. Some contemporary handmade damask is still made from silk, but many other types of cloth are also used.

What makes the fabric special is not only its elaborate and elegant designs, but the weave, which creates a raised pattern on both sides of the cloth—perhaps the world's first reversible material.

GLASS

Yet another Damascene specialty is hand-blown glass. This art form was invented over three thousand years ago by the Phoenicians. Today, there are few people in Syria who possess the knowledge of this unique profession. To blow glass, a glassblower picks up a piece of molten glass on the end of a long, hollow tube. Then, he or she gently blows air into the molten ball, making it bigger. As the glass cools, the glassblower uses tongs and other tools to shape it into an elaborate cup, jug, lamp, or light fixture. Colors are also added during this process.

This intricate process, however, has suffered in recent years, and the market in Syria for these handcrafted masterpieces has virtually disappeared. While thirty years ago, many Syrians purchased blown glass items, in recent years, the market had largely been sustained by tourism, until the war broke out in 2011. Today, there is little business left to sustain these artists' livelihood. However, in Damascus and a few other places, glassblowers continue to preserve this ancient art on a smaller scale amid the uncertainty of the future.

A glassblower in Damascus spins a molten ball of glass at the end of a long pipe.

INTERNET LINKS

www.bbc.co.uk/programmes/p035w98n
Watch this BBC documentary on the power of poetry, and read interviews with poets in Syria who are speaking out against the civil war.

www.theguardian.com/world/gallery/2013/aug/19/ali-ferzat-cartoons-in-pictures
View a gallery of exiled artist Ali Ferzat's political cartoons.

www.moc.gov.sy/index.php
This website features a list of news and events supported by Syria's Ministry of Culture.

www.youtube.com/watch?v=6TekbkovmzY
Watch Abu Talal, a glassblower in Damascus, create beautiful blown glass art.

LEISURE

Cars and people crowd a busy street in Damascus in 2009, before the civil war.

LEISURE IN SYRIA HAS TAKEN ON new meaning for many. In areas riddled with constant fighting, fear keeps many Syrians close to home. However, in relatively stable cities such as Damascus, life carries on as best it can. Whereas Syrians used to escape the confines of the city for the openness and fresh air of the countryside, today they largely remain in the safer streets of the country's urban centers.

POPULAR PASTIMES

Social activities generally involve either whole families, only men, only women, or women and children. Depending on the community, particularly in Islamic areas, certain public activities are unacceptable for women, such as socializing with men who are not relatives.

Many older men sit around for hours at the all-male tea houses, drinking tea or Turkish coffee, smoking the hubble bubble, and either talking together or playing Syria's favorite board game—a Turkish variety of backgammon. Even men who are tending shops spend their time doing these things when there are no customers.

Women, on the other hand, are usually on the streets only with their parents, husbands, and children. Most often, though, they are at

Amid the uncertainty of war, small gestures bring renewed hope to Syrians. In spring 2015, the Rabwah steam train resumed services in Damascus after being shut down for four years. Many excited Syrians attended the opening, waving the national flag.

During the week, the train carries commuters to and from work. It can carry about one hundred passengers, alleviating some of the traffic on Damascus's roads. However, come Friday morning, the bright yellow train is filled with smiling children and young people dancing the dabka, a folk dance. While the train once carried passengers to the countryside for weekend trips, today it only travels 2.2 miles (3.5 km) along the gorge of the Barada River. Areas farther up the track are under rebel control and do not allow for safe travel.

home working or shopping for their families while the men are on the streets socializing. Their leisure time is mostly limited to chatting with other women or family members.

OUT AND ABOUT

Lunch and dinner with friends or extended families are often major social events, with restaurants full until after midnight, particularly on Thursday evenings. During the warm months—from about May through October—dining is usually under the stars, since most restaurants are either partially or completely alfresco. Depending on the work people do, either lunch or dinner can be the biggest meal of the day. Whichever it is, Syrians often

The favorite pastime for Syrians is talking. They never seem to tire of it and it fills most of their leisure time. Men sit in coffeehouses and discuss politics over a cup of coffee or tea and a hubble bubble, while women stay at home and chat with family or neighbors. The art of conversation is well developed, and people are respected for their wit and humor.

Men like to engage in a kind of structured teasing, a verbal game of seeing who can come up with the most ingenious way of needling his opponent. An important aspect of the game is inventing an insult that is both clever and eloquently expressed. These verbal displays are rooted in the long tradition of rhetoric in classical Arabic poetry.

spend two or three hours socializing, eating, and drinking tea. Long dinners are especially common in the cities.

When Syrians go out for strolls in the streets and parks at night—something they do in hordes in nice weather—they wear their best clothing. Even conservative Muslim women often wear fashionable scarves and dresses. In summer, ice cream shops are particularly popular places, much like the old soda shops in the United States. For those who have money to spend, shopping is a favorite pastime and part of the nighttime socializing.

The National Opera in Damascus.

Hammams (hah-MAMs), or bathhouses, are remnants of the Ottoman Empire. They are found in the oldest sections of the cities and are common gathering places for middle-aged and older men. As they do in coffeehouses, men are likely to smoke their hubble bubbles here, while relaxing and enjoying a good conversation. In Aleppo, the famous Yalbougha an-Nasry bathhouse, built in the fifteenth century, has been heavily damaged in the conflict.

ARTS AND CULTURAL ACTIVITIES

Except for an occasional Hollywood drama, cinemas show soapy Egyptian or violent American and Asian movies. These are mostly attended by rowdy young men. Prior to 2010, a rare exception to this was the international film festival held in Damascus once every two years. This was a time when films from many countries were shown. Due to conflicts in the area, however, the film festival has not occurred in more recent years.

The more affluent Syrians own DVD players, and for them, watching movies is a source of entertainment that is second only to socializing.

In general, Syrians love music, and educated city dwellers particularly like concerts. Syrians enjoy a wide range of music, from classical European and classical Arabic to Western jazz and Indian pop or folk music. Western bands, such as One Direction, are also popular with Syrian youths.

Syria has a National Symphony that performs several times a year at the Damascus Opera House, usually in front of a packed audience.

PHYSICAL RECREATION

Few Syrians engage in athletic activities or exercise of any kind. A few people hunt birds or foxes and gazelles in the desert, but this is more for food than for "sport." Fishing is also rare and done primarily either for food or as a job.

Some Syrians who live near Lake Al-Assad use the lake for fishing and recreation. Swimming in the lake on hot days and rowing small rowboats are the main activities.

SOCCER IN SYRIA

In Syria, soccer is known as football and is the country's most popular sport. Syria's national team is a member of the Fédération Internationale de Football Association (FIFA) and is working toward securing a berth in the 2018 World Cup. Syria also has its own league within the country made up of eight teams. The league is overseen by the Syrian Football Association, founded in 1936.

Due to the dangers posed by the civil war, the national team plays home games in different capital cities across the Middle East.

Even on the soccer field, political lines are being drawn; some players have left the country and joined a team based in Lebanon that hopes to one day be Syria's new national team, playing under a free and democratic flag. In a small act of protest, this team dresses in green, a color associated with those who oppose the Assad government.

INTERNET LINKS

www.bbc.com/news/world-middle-east-26577626
This BBC video offers a glimpse at life in Damascus three years into the Syrian civil war.

www.fifa.com/associations/association=syr
Learn all about football in Syria on the FIFA website.

www.youtube.com/watch?v=DZMPmAW1XFQ
Listen to a stirring performance by the Syrian National Symphony.

FESTIVALS

The camel races at Palmyra covered a distance of 3 miles (5 km).

12

A S A PREDOMINANTLY MUSLIM country, most celebrations in Syria are religious in nature. Other holidays mark important events in the country's tumultuous past, or celebrations unique to minority groups living there.

Chief Muslim holidays are Eid al-Fitr at the end of the fasting month of Ramadan, and Eid al-Adha at the end of the hajj. Christmas and Easter are celebrated by Christians, but there are not many community festivities for these holidays. Christians usually have a quiet family celebration for holidays, although some decorations appear in shops around the Christmas season.

Important anniversaries, which reflect the sense of Syrian national identity following independence, are Revolution Day on March 8,

The Tomb of the Unknown Soldier in Damascus.

During the spring, the Palmyra Desert Festival traditionally drew many visitors to the city's ancient ruins. The festivities included cultural music and dance performances, foods, handicrafts, and horse and camel races.

New Year's Day	*January 1*
Revolution Day	*March 8*
Mother's Day	*March 21*
National Day	*April 17*
Labor Day	*May 1*
Martyr's Day	*May 6*
Liberation War Day	*October 6*
National Day of Mourning	*November 29*
Christmas Day	*December 25*

the Birth of the Arab League on March 22, the commemoration of French withdrawal on April 17, Martyr's Day on May 6, and the National Day of Mourning on November 29.

REMEMBERING SYRIA'S HISTORY

Celebrations on Revolution Day commemorate the anniversary of the 1963 revolution when the Baath Party came into power as the head of the Syrian government. On this day, the government traditionally holds rallies with officials making speeches, and parades take place in cities such as Damascus. On Independence Day, also called National Day, Syrian flags are proudly flown. This public holiday celebrates the end of the French occupation in Syria, when Syria officially gained its independence. On Martyr's Day, political patriots who died fighting for Syrian independence from the Ottoman Empire are remembered.

HOLY DAYS

All Muslim festivals vary in date from year to year. The Islamic calendar is based on the phases of the moon, and so has only 354 days. This means that the major festivals occur eleven or twelve days earlier each year compared

A Syrian family breaks the fast during *iftar*.

with the calendar used in the United States and Europe. The dates for Eid al-Fitr and Eid al-Adha are determined by the sighting of the new moon and occur at different times in Islamic countries that are distant from each other.

RAMADAN Ramadan is the ninth month of the Islamic calendar. During Ramadan, Muslims fast from sunrise until sunset. From the first light of day until the imam can no longer distinguish between a white and a black thread in natural light, Muslims refrain from eating or drinking. This can become difficult if Ramadan falls during hot weather, and young children, the elderly, the sick, travelers, soldiers, and women who are menstruating are excused from fasting, although they must make it up later. People often become very tired during the fast, and life generally slows down. Ramadan is a time for Muslims to focus their attention on spiritual matters, and many families put aside time to read the Qur'an. The act of fasting proves their devotion to the Prophet Muhammad and Allah. It also builds self-discipline and instills compassion for those less fortunate.

Syrian Kurds welcome the first day of spring with the celebration of Nōrūz, which translates from Persian to "new day." The festival takes place on March 21, the spring equinox. People dress in brightly colored clothing, enjoy outdoor picnics, and perform traditional dances.

Kurdish legend tells the story of Kowa, the son of a blacksmith. He slayed a giant who terrorized his people and ate children. At Nōrūz celebrations, fires are lit to symbolize Kurdish independence in the face of oppression. Most Kurds are also Sunni Muslims and celebrate traditional Islamic holidays as well as ones that reflect their unique heritage.

The celebration comes with the *iftar*, or evening meal, that breaks the day's fast. Food is set on the table in vast quantities, and the family is seated and ready to feast on the food as soon as the minarets sound the end of the day's fast. Once the eating starts, no one says anything for a while, and unlike regular meals, which often drag on for an hour or more, the food is gone in minutes!

Iftar is made special not only by the hunger that builds up during daylight hours, but by special foods, the sheer quantity of food, and the presence of extended family.

EID AL-FITR Eid al-Fitr marks the end of Ramadan, and people stuff themselves on special foods (especially sweets), stay up all night, and spend time visiting with extended families and friends. People traditionally wear new clothes during Eid al-Fitr. It is also customary for children to get money from their uncles. Eid al-Fitr officially lasts only three days, but if those days fall midweek, some shops, schools, and embassies remain closed the entire week.

On September 13, 2015, a new festival organized by Syria's Ministry of Culture and officials from the province of Latakia was held. Entitled Syria Stronger, the month-long celebration included a market for shopping and artistic, acrobatic, athletic, and gymnastic performances. The provincial governor explained the celebration's goal, saying, "Holding the festival conveys a message on the resilience of the Syrian people and their determination to life the [sic] with all its sweet and bitter details." In the future, the festival hopes to work with other cultural organizations within Syria.

EID AL-ADHA Eid al-Adha is celebrated in about the same manner as Eid al-Fitr. It comes at the traditional end of hajj and celebrates the near-sacrifice of Ishmael (who is called Isaac by Christians) by his father, Abraham. During Eid al-Adha, almost nothing is open—government or private.

INTERNET LINKS

www.iexplore.com/travel-guides/middle-east/syria/festivals-and-events
This site lists festivals celebrated in Syria.

www.war-memorial.net/The-Tomb-of-the-Unknown-Soldier-(Damascus)-1.304
Learn more about Damascus's Tomb of the Unknown Soldier here.

FOOD

A plate of *kibbeh* is often served alongside yogurt and flatbread.

13

FOOD AND WARM HOSPITALITY LIE at the heart of daily life in Syria. Meals are traditionally long, often taking hours to complete. Each city and region in Syria brings its own unique flavors to the country's cuisine. Many of these dishes showcase foods harvested from the area, such as pistachios from Aleppo's famous orchards or the tangy pepper named for the city. The Syrian palate includes foods that range from extremely sweet to immensely sour and are richly flavored with spices.

However, since the war began in 2011, many of these traditional flavors have become a distant memory for the millions of Syrians who now lack daily access to food. For those Syrians who have fled around the globe, traditional dishes provide a much-loved taste of home.

FOODS OF THE MIDDLE EAST

Syrian cuisine is similar to that of other Middle Eastern countries. Some dishes have become popular around the world. Hummus, an appetizer made by blending sesame paste and chickpeas, and tabouleh, a salad made of bulgur (cracked wheat) mixed with tomatoes and parsley, are

A bowl of tabouleh.

two examples. Falafels, patties made of ground chickpeas, have also made their way into Western countries, as well as the flat round breads called pitas. Baba ganouj, a mashed eggplant dish, is another export.

STAPLES OF THE SYRIAN CHEF

Whether served at home or at a restaurant, Syrian food uses essentially the same ingredients: lots of lamb, chicken, dried beans (especially chickpeas), eggplant, rice, and bulgur. Additionally, olives, yogurt, and Syrian cheese (a white, usually salty cheese most often made from goat's or sheep's milk) are commonly part of meals. There are dozens of varieties of olives, ranging from enormous to tiny, from yellow to jet black, from bitter and dry to sweet and juicy, and from crunchy to soft. Garlic and olive oil (or purified butterfat) are also used heavily in or on most foods. Coffee or tea follows every meal.

EATING TRADITIONS

Some common food practices in Syria include:

- Muslims traditionally do not use their left hand when eating, since the Qur'an dictates that the left is to be used for the toilet.
- For Syrian Muslims, certain food restrictions apply. Islam forbids the consumption of pork or alcohol, and meats must be specially prepared in a halal way.
- It is traditional for the host to insist that the guest eat more until everything on the table is gone.
- Most food is eaten by hand or scooped up with bits of flatbread, but French fries are eaten with a fork.

- French fries are the only form of potatoes eaten, and they accompany every restaurant meal.
- All flatbread dips are drizzled with olive oil and garnished with fresh parsley or mint.

THREE MEALS A DAY

For those who eat breakfast, it often comes quite early—school days start at 6 a.m. during the heat of summer, and devout Muslims get up before dawn to pray. Lunch, the largest meal for most people, is around 2 p.m. and is followed by a siesta. Except for special occasions, dinner is usually light and always eaten late; in fact, most restaurants do not open until 8 p.m. and stay open until midnight or later.

Meals range from a light breakfast of olives, cheese, yogurt, and Turkish coffee to special family dinners with dozens of dishes. The main meal consists of a soup (lentil is a favorite), a stew made from chicken or lamb,

Men enjoy a cup of strong Turkish coffee.

The World Food Programme (WFP) is one of many organizations working to address the growing food shortage within Syria's borders by supplying food to more than four million displaced men, women, and children. Due to a critical shortage in funding, many of these refugees survive on around 50 cents a day.

Some of the WFP's assistance includes:

- *Three thousand trucks within the country are sent to make the dangerous trek to deliver much needed rations to displaced families, including rice, bulgur wheat, pasta, lentils, canned food, sugar, salt, cooking oil, and wheat flour.*

- *Forty thousand tons (36,287 t) of food are delivered within Syria each month.*

- *Working with UNICEF and the Syrian Ministry of Education, nutritious date bars are provided to 164,000 schoolchildren.*

- *As of October 2015, electronic vouchers provide $21 monthly to each Syrian refugee in neighboring countries to cover the cost of food.*

- *Some Syrians have remained in the country and are working with nonprofit organizations. Rawda al-Khouli is one of many Syrians working on the frontlines delivering food for the WFP. For al-Khouli, her purpose is simple: "These are my people. I am making a difference."*

salads, appetizers of various sorts, different kinds of stuffed pastries, cooked vegetables, bread, and fruit for dessert. It is nearly always accompanied by trays of olives and very sour pickles. A late supper might include olives, cheese, yogurt, bread, and tea.

Syrians make some special foods—a few in large enough batches to last most of a year. One such item is small eggplants stuffed with spiced meat that are then pickled. Small zucchini-type squash are also stuffed with a rice-meat mixture but not pickled. Yet another favorite is artichoke hearts stuffed with spicy meat and pine nuts.

SIMPLE TOOLS

Syrian kitchens in middle- and upper-class homes are similar to, but not as elaborate as, middle-class American kitchens. Few Syrians have such luxuries as dishwashers, food processors, microwaves, and meat grinders. Poorer Syrians—who comprise most of the population—get by with basic utensils and a lot of hard work in the kitchen. For example, garlic is bought in large bunches and first chopped, then crushed in a mortar and pestle. All this work falls to the women of the family, particularly the mother, because few Syrian men know how to cook.

A Syrian woman can choose from a rich variety of spices at a souk.

BUYING FOOD

Most groceries are bought fresh every day. In modern families, the whole family may share the shopping chores. This is necessary because not many Syrians have cars, and the quantity of food needed by a large family is vast.

Food shopping in Syria is time consuming because there is a separate shop for each type of food. There are even four different types of bakeries: one bakes only flatbread, a Syrian staple; another bakes baguettes and sandwich rolls; another creates elaborately decorated European-style pastries; and the fourth makes Syrian specialties—dense, rich confections with heavy use of pistachios and sugar water.

In addition to larger shops, there are many street-corner kiosks that sell candies, toiletries, magazines, and newspapers. In some neighborhoods, fresh local produce can be bought from farmers who trek through with their donkeys or horse-drawn carts, chanting their lists of goods.

EATING OUT

Syrian food is similar, whether it is prepared in Aleppo, Damascus, or Deir ez-Zor. The only difference is that some dishes vary slightly in texture, flavor, and spiciness. Standard dishes are grilled lamb or chicken; a Syrian specialty called kibbeh (KIB-beh), a delicious meat pie made with ground lamb, bulgar, pine nuts, and seasonings; *boorak* (BOO-rok), a cheese-filled pastry; *yalangi* (ya-LAWN-gee), grape leaves stuffed with seasoned rice; various dips made from beans, seeds, yogurt, eggplant, and hot peppers; flatbread to eat the dips with; and various kinds of salads, including tabouleh, a Middle Eastern specialty. The menu is the same for breakfast, lunch, and dinner, except for a few things, such as *fool* (fava beans cooked in oil, lemon juice, and garlic, then topped with yogurt) and *fatteh* (a slightly sour concoction similar to hot breakfast cereal), which are eaten for breakfast. There is always a tray of pickles, olives, mint, and raw vegetables—usually radishes and green peppers.

A market bakery displays towers of puff pastries.

Only a few restaurants serve fish, and it is quite expensive. The Mediterranean off the coast of Syria is not rich in seafood and has no harvest of shellfish.

Also, few restaurants serve alcohol, but carbonated soft drinks are immensely popular, and Syrians drink them with all meals—even breakfast! They call it all "cola."

FOODS TO GO

There are a few Western-style fast food franchises in Syria, but the country has its own kinds of fast food. All Syrian cities have small shops that make a sort of Syrian burrito called shawarma (SHAH-war-ma). This is thinly sliced lamb or chicken with garnishes rolled up in a small piece of flatbread. Another type of shop sells falafel sandwiches—crumbled falafel mixed with yogurt, parsley, and other items and also rolled up in flat bread. Chicken shops sell

With plentiful rain showers, the spring brings a bountiful crop of kemeh, or desert truffles, to the sands of Syria. Although found across the Middle East, many believe that the highly prized truffles originated in Syria, near the ruins of Palmyra. This delicacy is harvested by the desert-dwelling Bedouins, who sell the truffles in city markets.

The truffles grow under the sand, near rockroses. As they increase in size, telltale bumps appear in the sand. According to Bedouin tradition, if there are several lightning storms in November and December, a good crop of "the potatoes of thunder" will follow in the spring. If not, it is wise to wait until the following year. Sometimes five years can pass without a crop of kemeh.

Kemeh are a member of the mushroom family and are an excellent source of protein. Their flavor is described as a cross between a mushroom and an artichoke. To cook, they must be soaked in water and rinsed many times to remove sand that is trapped in their gnarled exterior. They can be cooked in a number of ways: boiled, fried, added to traditional dishes like kebabs, or served in a simple salad, dressed in olive oil and coriander.

whole roasted birds stuffed with rice or cracked wheat mixtures as well as fried chicken.

Starting in early spring, there are decorated carts on street corners that sell unripened almonds, a sour treat dipped in salt. After the season for almonds is over, the vendors sell unripened plums that look similar to green cherry tomatoes. The cart venders also sell corn on the cob. On hot summer evenings, people taking their nightly strolls munch on the corn. A few carts also offer coconuts and roasted chestnuts.

If you have ever had the pleasure of dining out in a real Mediterranean restaurant, you may have encountered the meze, or mazza *in Arabic. This is a huge platter of small tasty snacks that sometimes precedes the main meal but can be a meal in itself. The Syrian mazza usually includes flatbreads like pita served with* hummus *(mashed chickpeas with garlic and oil),* baba ganouj *(eggplant with sesame paste), and* mouhammara *(minced meat with onions and nuts, wrapped in breadcrumbs and oatmeal). Mazzas only include savory foods and, though they are served in small portions, there is a wide variety so that you can quickly fill up. Dining out in Syria in the evening almost always involves a mazza before the main meal.*

The mazza is a pan-Mediterranean custom spanning European countries like Spain with its tapas, Italy with its antipasti, Greece, Turkey, and continuing around the Mediterranean to the Middle East and parts of North Africa. Whether they're the first course or the main meal, mazzas are an excellent way to sample the key spices and ingredients of the local cuisine.

In late summer, street-corner stands are put up to sell ripe prickly pears, and the stand owner peels them so that the customer can eat the delicious fruit without the stickers.

Finally, there are hundreds of juice shops where fresh juice or juice and milk drinks are made and served by the bottle or glass. Banana milk and strawberry milk are favorites.

ROOTED IN TRADITION

The Syrian people, as a rule, are extremely picky about what they eat, and most of them do not even like to try different kinds of food. An exception to this is that many city dwellers (especially teenagers) like pizza, hamburgers, and hot dogs, although these are noticeably different from those in the United States.

As in most other arts, tradition rules in cooking. An example: Yogurt is a large part of the diet, used in several different types of dips, as a topping on various dishes, and as a drink mixed with water, salt, and garlic. Syrians even eat plain yogurt by itself. Yet the idea of mixing it with fruit in a blender to make a drink, eating it with fruit or jam mixed in, or using it on a baked potato sounds disgusting to most Syrians. They believe that yogurt should only be eaten the way they have traditionally eaten it.

A Syrian vendor sells fresh falafel from his street stall.

INTERNET LINKS

www.foodandwine.com/articles/the-syrian-pantry
A list of staple foods and spices found in the Syrian kitchen, including links to recipes using each unique ingredient.

www.theguardian.com/travel/2008/aug/24/damascus. travelfoodanddrink
This travel article takes readers on a culinary tour through the flavors and souks of Syria.

www.sbs.com.au/food/article/2009/01/21/about-syrian-food
This site gives an overview of Syrian cuisine and its traditional dishes.

www.wfp.org/emergencies/syria
This website discusses WFP's assistance to Syria's displaced people.

SHORBAT ADAS (LENTIL SOUP)

2 tablespoons (30 milliliters) of extra virgin olive oil
1 onion, finely chopped
1 carrot, finely chopped
1 celery stalk, including the leaves, fincly chopped
2 teaspoons (5 grams) of cumin
¼ teaspoon (1 g) of cinnamon
½ pound (227 g) of dried lentils
5 cups (1.2 liters) of vegetable or chicken stock, or water
1 bunch of swiss chard, roughly chopped with the stems removed
2 tablespoons (30 mL) of lemon juice
salt and pepper

In a large stock pot, heat the olive oil. Add the chopped onion, carrot, and celery, and cook for about 8 minutes, or until soft. Stir in the cumin and cinnamon and allow to cook for 1 minute. Add in the stock or water, then the dried lentils. Bring to a boil, then cover and simmer over low-medium heat. After about 20 minutes, once the lentils are tender, add the swiss chard. Stir in the lemon juice and season to taste with salt and pepper. Makes four servings.

BARAZEH (SESAME SEED COOKIES)

¼ cup (38 g) of sesame seeds
½ tablespoon (7 mL) of honey
½ tablespoon (7 mL) of water
2 ½ cups (330 g) of flour, sifted
½ teaspoon (2 g) of baking powder
¾ cup (175 g) of sugar
¾ cup (170 g) unsalted butter, softened
Đ cup (79 mL) of water

Preheat the oven to 350°F (176°C). Spread the sesame seeds in a single layer on a baking sheet and toast until golden brown. Carefully pour the toasted seeds into a small dish. Moisten the seeds by adding one-half tablespoon of honey and one-half tablespoon of water.

In a large mixing bowl, combine the flour, baking power, and sugar. With a butter knife, carefully cut the butter in small pieces into the dry ingredients. Slowly add in the water until a smooth ball of dough forms.

Form the dough into small balls, about the size of a walnut. Then, gently press the ball into the sesame seeds, coating the top. Place the cookies on a greased cookie sheet and bake until golden brown, approximately 15 to 20 minutes.

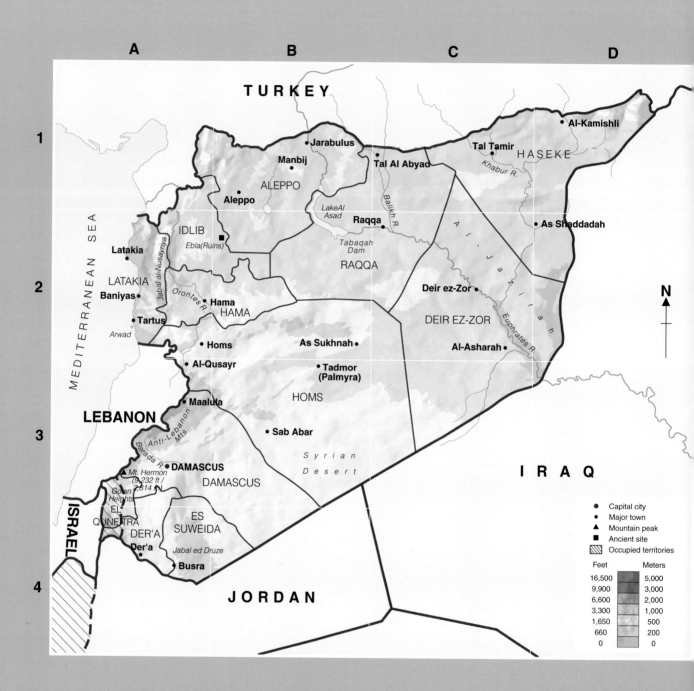

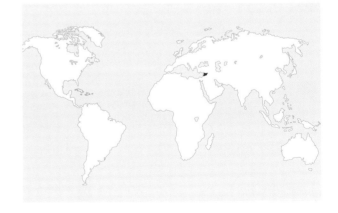

ECONOMIC SYRIA

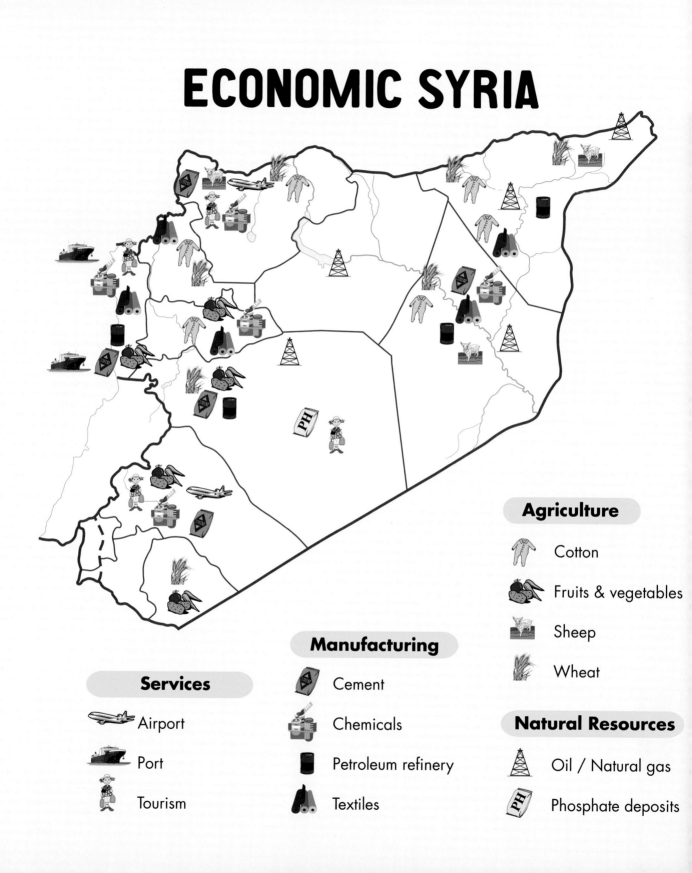

Services

- ✈ Airport
- 🚢 Port
- 🧍 Tourism

Manufacturing

- Cement
- Chemicals
- Petroleum refinery
- Textiles

Agriculture

- Cotton
- Fruits & vegetables
- Sheep
- Wheat

Natural Resources

- Oil / Natural gas
- Phosphate deposits

ABOUT THE ECONOMY

OVERVIEW

Syria's economy has suffered greatly since the onset of the civil war in 2011. In 2014, the economy further suffered under international sanctions, a crumbling national infrastructure, and rising inflation. The added strain of the humanitarian crisis within the country has necessitated assistance from the international community.

GROSS DOMESTIC PRODUCT

US $64.7 billion (2011 estimate)

GDP PER CAPITA

$5,100 (2011)

GDP SECTORS

Agriculture 18.1 percent; industry 19 percent; services 62.9 percent (2014 estimate)

CURRENCY

1 Syrian pound (SYP) = 100 piastres
USD 1 = SYP 188.79 (October 2015)
Notes: 5, 10, 25, 50, 100, 200, 500, 1000 SYP
Coins: 1, 2, 5, 10, 25 piastres (no longer issued)

ECONOMIC GROWTH RATE

—2.3 percent (2011)

LABOR FORCE

4.022 million (2014 estimate)

UNEMPLOYMENT RATE

33 percent (2014 estimate)

INFLATION RATE

34.8 percent (2014 estimate)

IMPORTS

Machinery and transport equipment, electric power machinery, food and livestock, metal and metal products, chemicals and chemical products, plastics, yarn, paper

EXPORTS

Crude oil, minerals, petroleum products, fruits and vegetables, cotton fiber, textiles, clothing, meat and live animals, wheat

MAJOR TRADE PARTNERS

Iraq, Saudi Arabia, Kuwait, Turkey, United Arab Emirates, Iran, China, Libya (2014)

OIL RESERVES

2.500 million barrels (2015)

CRUDE OIL PRODUCTION

25,000 barrels/day (2015)

INDUSTRIES

Petroleum, textiles, processed food, beverages, tobacco, phosphate rock mining, cement, oil seeds crushing, automobile assembly

AGRICULTURAL PRODUCTS

Wheat, barley, cotton, lentils, chickpeas, olives, sugar beets, beef, mutton, eggs, poultry, milk

CULTURAL SYRIA

Aleppo Citadel
The city of Aleppo is renowned for Islamic military architecture of the twelfth and thirteenth centuries including Aleppo Citadel built by the son of Saladin in the middle of the city.

Water Wheels
The city of Hama is famous for its ancient water wheels.

Cave Houses
The city of Maaloula has the greatest concentration of cave houses where people still speak Aramaic, the language of Jesus

World Heritage Site
Queen Zenobia's palace and other Roman ruins are being excavated here, in the city of Palmyra.

**Al Talila
(just outside Palmyra)**
First wildlife refuge in the country.

Christian Churches
Homs also has many churches, some like St. Elian, boasting frescoes dating back to the twelfth century.

Omayyad Mosque
The famous Omayyad Mosque in Damascus was built 1300 years ago when Islam first spread to Syria.

National Museum
Damascus is home to many museums including the National Museum. It is also the site of some of the oldest souks, or markets featuring Syrian crafts like Damasc brocades, copper and woodwork.

Krak des Chevaliers
This castle found in the city of Homs was built by the Crusaders and is considered to be one of the most magnificent castles in the world.

ABOUT THE CULTURE

OFFICIAL NAME
Syrian Arab Republic

NATIONAL FLAG
Three equal horizontal bands of red (top), white (middle), and black (bottom); two small green five-pointed stars centered in a line in the white band.

NATIONAL ANTHEM
"Homat el Diyar" ("Guardians of the Homeland")

POPULATION
17,064,854 (July 2014)

POPULATION GROWTH RATE
—0.16 percent (2015)

LITERACY
86.4 percent

CAPITAL
Damascus

OTHER MAJOR CITIES
Aleppo, Homs, Lattakia, Hama, Al-Kamishli, Rakka, Deir ez-Zor, Tartous

GOVERNMENT
Republic under an authoritarian regime

OFFICIAL LANGUAGE
Arabic (official); Kurdish, Armenian, Aramaic, Circassian widely understood; French, English somewhat understood

LIFE EXPECTANCY AT BIRTH
74.69 years

RELIGION
Muslim 87 percent (official; 74 percent Sunni, 13 percent Alawite, Ismaili, and Shia), 10 percent Christian, 3 percent Druze, some Jewish remain in Damascus and Aleppo

ADMINISTRATIVE REGIONS
14 provinces: Al Hasakah, Al Ladhiqiyah, Al Qunaytirah, Ar Raqqah, As Suwayda', Der'a, Dayr az Zawr, Dimashq, Halab, Hamah, Hims, Idlib, Rif Dimashq, Tartus

ETHNIC GROUPS
Arabs 90.3 percent; Kurds, Armenians, and others 9.7 percent

TIMELINE

IN SYRIA	IN THE WORLD
1200 BCE The Aramaean kingdom is established in Syria.	
	753 BCE Rome is founded.
64 BCE Romans, led by Pompey the Great, conquer Syria.	
	116–117 CE The Roman Empire reaches its greatest extent, under Emperor Trajan (98–117).
	600 CE Height of Mayan civilization.
636 CE Omayyad Arabs conquer Damascus and introduce Islam to Syria.	**1000** The Chinese perfect gunpowder and begin to use it in warfare.
1096 French Crusaders occupy parts of Syria.	
1174 Saladin occupies Syria. His heirs, the Ayyubids, bring stability to the region.	
1516 Ottoman Turks take control of Syria.	
	1530 Beginning of transatlantic slave trade organized by the Portuguese in Africa.
	1558–1603 Reign of Elizabeth I of England.
	1620 Pilgrims sail the *Mayflower* to America.
	1776 US Declaration of Independence.
	1789–1799 The French Revolution.
	1861 The US Civil War begins.
	1914 World War I begins.
1918 Arab troops, supported by British forces, capture Damascus, ending four hundred years of Ottoman rule.	
1920 San Remo international conference places Syria and Lebanon under the French forces.	**1939** World War II begins.

IN SYRIA		IN THE WORLD
1940		
Syria comes under the Axis powers following the fall of France to German forces.		
1946–1947		
British and French troops leave Syria, and the Arab Socialist Baath Party is founded.	**1949**	
	NATO is formed.	
	1957	
1958	The Russians launch *Sputnik 1*.	
Syria and Egypt join the United Arab Republic.		
1963		
A new Baathist-dominated cabinet is appointed. Amin al-Hafez becomes president.	**1966–1969**	
	The Chinese Cultural Revolution.	
1970–1971		
Hafez al-Assad is elected president.	**1980–1981**	
1982–1983	Start of Iran–Iraq War. Israel formally annexes the Golan Heights.	
Israel invades Lebanon and attacks the Syrian army. After the end of hostilities, Syrian forces remain in Lebanon.	**1986**	
	Nuclear power disaster at Chernobyl.	
1990		
Following the Iraqi invasion of Kuwait, Syria joins the US-led coalition against Iraq.	**1991**	
	Breakup of the Soviet Union.	
	1997	
	Hong Kong is returned to China.	
2000		
President Assad dies and is succeeded by his son, Bashar.		
2001	**2001**	
Government approves private banks for the first time. Pope John Paul II visits Syria. Syria elected to seat on UN Security Council.	Terrorists crash planes in New York, Washington, DC, and Pennsylvania.	
	2003	
2005	War in Iraq.	
Syria claims it has withdrawn all its military forces from Lebanon.		
2011		
Civil war breaks out in Syria.		
2014	**2014**	
ISIL expands and declares a caliphate in its territory in Iraq and Syria.	Russia invades Ukraine.	

GLOSSARY

caliph
The title given to a descendent of the Islamic Prophet Muhammad who acts as the spiritual leader of the Muslim faith.

caliphate
An Islamic state ruled by a caliph who is given absolute power and authority.

Eid al-Adha (ah-EED al AD-thah)
The Muslim festival that occurs at the end of hajj, celebrating Abraham's near-sacrifice of his son Isaac.

Eid al-Fitr (ah-EED al FIT-ur)
The Muslim festival that occurs at the end of Ramadan, celebrating the breaking of the fast.

hajj (haaj)
A pilgrimage to Mecca, one of the five pillars of Islam.

halal
The slaughter and preparation of an animal following rules outlined in the holy Qur'an.

iftar
The evening meal that breaks the daily fast during Ramadan.

insha'Allah (in-SHAH-al-LAH)
A common Arabic expression, meaning "God willing."

kaffiyeh (ku-FEE-yea)
A wrapped cotton headdress frequently worn by Syrian men.

Ramadan (RAH-mah-dan)
The ninth month of the Islamic calendar, during which Muslims fast from sunrise to sunset.

salat (sa-LAAT)
Prayer five times daily, one of the five pillars of Islam.

sawm (soom)
Fasting during Ramadan, one of the five pillars of Islam.

shahada (sha-HAA-da)
The declaration that there is only one God and that Muhammad was his last prophet, one of the five pillars of Islam.

Sharia (shah-ree-AH)
The Muslim code, a legal system based on the prescriptions of the Qur'an.

Shia (SHEE-ah)
A Muslim sect believing in the divine right of the caliphs.

souk (sook)
A traditional marketplace.

Sunni (SOON-ee)
A Muslim sect believing in election of the caliphs.

zakat (za-CAT)
An annual tithe of 2.5 percent of earnings above basic necessities, one of the five pillars of Islam.

FOR FURTHER INFORMATION

BOOKS

Halasa, Malu, Zaher Omareen, and Nawara Mahfoud, eds. *Syria Speaks: Art and Culture from the Frontline*. London: Saqi Books, 2014.

Imady, Muna. *Syrian Folktales*. Hollister, CA: MSI Press, 2012.

Massaud, Barbara Abdeni. *Soup for Syria: Recipes to Celebrate our Shared Humanity*. Northampton, MA: Interlink Books, 2015.

Monaghan, Louise. *Stolen: Escape from Syria*. New York: St. Martin's Press, 2012.

Sahner, Christian. *Among the Ruins: Syria Past and Present*. London: Hurst Publishers, 2014.

Weiss, Michael, and Hassan Hassan. *ISIS: Inside the Army of Terror*. New York: Regan Arts, 2015.

Yazbek, Samar. *The Crossing: My Journey to the Shattered Heart of Syria*. London: Ebury Press, 2016.

Yomtov, Nel. *Syria*. Enchantment of the World. New York: Scholastic, 2013.

Zahler, Kathy A. *The Assads' Syria*. Dictatorships. Minneapolis, MN: Lerner Publishing, 2009.

FILM

Frontline: The Rise of the Isis. PBS, 2014 (DVD).

Frontline: Syria Behind the Lines. PBS, 2013 (DVD).

WEBSITES

Aljazeera. http://www.aljazeera.com/topics/country/syria.html

BBC News Country Profiles: Syria. http://news.bbc.co.uk/1/hi/world/middle_east/country_profiles/827580.stm

Central Intelligence Agency World Factbook: Syria. https://www.cia.gov/library/publications/the-world-factbook/geos/sy.html

New York Times: Syria. http://topics.nytimes.com/top/news/international/countriesand territories/syria/index.html

Syrian Cooking. http://syriancooking.com

USAID: Crisis in Syria. http://www.usaid.gov/crisis/syria

BIBLIOGRAPHY

Almasri. Radwan, Tariq Muneer, and Kevin Cullinane. "The effect of transport on air quality in urban areas of Syria." Elsevier. May 2, 2011. BBC News. "Golan Heights profile." November 27, 2015. http://www.bbc.com/news/world-middle-east-14724842.

BBC News. "Who, What, Why: Who are the Yazidis?" August 8, 2014. http://www.bbc.com/news/blogs-magazine-monitor-28686607?ocid=socialflow_gplus.

Black, Ian. "Endangered Aramaic language makes a comeback in Syria." *The Guardian*. April 14, 2009. http://www.theguardian.com/world/2009/apr/14/aramaic-revival-syria.

Carnegie Endowment for International Peace. "The Damascus Spring." http://carnegieendowment.org/syriaincrisis/?fa=48516.

Dorsey, James M. "Syrian Soccer: Succeeding Against the Odds." Aljazeera America. October 9, 2009. http://america.aljazeera.com/articles/2015/10/9/syrian-soccer-succeeding-against-the-odds.html.

Encyclopaedia Britannica. "Bashar al-Assad." http://www.britannica.com/biography/Bashar-al-Assad.

Gilsinan, Kathy. "The Confused Person's Guide to the Syrian Civil War." *The Atlantic*. October 29, 2015. http://www.theatlantic.com/international/archive/2015/10/syrian-civil-war-guide-isis/410746.

Landais, Emmanuelle. "Desert truffles are few and far between." *Gulf News*. February 26, 2009. http://gulfnews.com/news/uae/environment/desert-truffles-are-few-and-far-between-1.53509.

Shamout, M. Nouar, and Glada Lahn. "The Euphrates in Crisis: Channels of Cooperation for a Threatened River." Chatham House. April 2015. http://www.chathamhouse.org/sites/files/chathamhouse/field/field_document/20150413Euphrates_0.pdf.

Stelfox, Dave. "Ali Ferzat, cartoonist in exile." *The Guardian*. August 19, 2012. http://www.theguardian.com/world/2013/aug/19/ali-ferzat-cartoonist-exile-syria.

US Energy Information Administration. Syria: International Energy Data and Analysis. http://www.eia.gov/beta/international/analysis.cfm?iso=SYR.

Zein Alabadin, Mahmoud. "The Courtyard Houses of Syria." Muslim Heritage. http://www.muslimheritage.com/article/courtyard-houses-syria.

INDEX

INDEX